THE COMPLETE 7 KATAS OF JUDO

THE COMPLETE
7 KATAS OF JUDO

By

Mikonosuke KAWAISHI Shihan
7th Dan
TECHNICAL DIRECTOR
OF THE
FRENCH FEDERATION OF JUDO

Translated and edited by
E. J. HARRISON 4th Dan

Adaptation and Drawings by
JEAN GAILHAT

THE OVERLOOK PRESS
Woodstock, New York

First published in the United States in 1982 by
The Overlook Press
Lewis Hollow Road
Woodstock, New York 12498

Copyright © 1957 by M. Kawaishi
First published in England by W. Foulsham & Co. Ltd.

Library of Congress Cataloging in Publication Data

Kawaishi, Mikinosuke.
   The complete 7 katas of judo.

   Translation of: Les katas complets de judo.
   Reprint. Originally published: London :
W. Foulsham, 1957.
   1. Judo. I. Title. II. Title: Complete seven
katas of judo.
GV1114.K3813 1982   796.8'152   82-3470
ISBN 0-87951-156-7   AACR2

Printed in the USA

CONTENTS

AUTHOR'S FOREWORD

IN Japanese the word "KATA" signifies "fundamental or basic form". Although in Japanese the same character serves for both singular and plural numbers, it has been deemed advisable in the interests of non-Japanese readers to indicate the plural in the text by adding an "s" to the word Kata.

A KATA OF JUDO is the demonstration of a fundamental or basic interdependent form of attack and defence.

The party who throws and defends himself is called TORI, he who executes and demonstrates the relevant method. The attacker is called UKE, i.e. he who finally submits. These terms are somewhat arbitrary and at first sight confusing. Literally TORI means Taker and UKE Receiver. The point is that UKE, the formal assailant, is always defeated and succumbs to TORI's counter-attack.

TORI and UKE must resolutely execute and demonstrate the chosen movements, and in so doing completely and efficaciously utilize all their mental and physical energy in conformity with the great ideal of Judo which consists in the maximum employment of one's capacities directed to a fixed purpose through the application of the technique of Judo.

In the Katas we should find exemplified the three basic principles of Judo, viz., (1) The optimum employment of energy, i.e. the maximum of efficacy combined with the minimum of effort, or in Japanese "Seiryoku Zenyō"; (2) Mutual aid, mutual prosperity and amelioration which are the contemplated aim or "Jita Kyoei". The Kata is team work with care and personal improvement and of conclusive and educational value; (3) The "manner" and the Judo technique which consists in lithely giving way in order better to conquer.

The customary movements of the different Katas which follow in a rigorous progression are the result of century-old experience and profound reflection of the best and oldest Masters. All the holds, all the positions down to their smallest detail have been meticulously chosen, improved and classified to result in a definitive shape, perfected, true, the most beautiful, the purest and most representative of the spirit and ideal of Judo.

Another merit should be recognized for the Katas, which is by no means negligible: that of having preserved and transmitted the tradition of the old techniques of Jujutsu,

7

even when certain abuses have rendered Jujutsu rather un-
popular in Japan, and have thus contributed in no small
degree to the creation and development of Judo.

In old Japan Judo did not exist, so that the art is barely
75 years of age.

But JUJUTSU, its ancestor, knew many Katas, such as the
KOSHIKI-NO-KATA, which constituted the "exercises of style"
of which it may even be said that the practice bore a
quasi-religious character, in any case clearly mystical and
which at the same time aimed at setting off the beauty of
gesture and at showing that the performer had perfectly
assimilated, in the first place, the spiritual mastery, then the
technique of combat thus illustrated in its martial whole and
in each of its processes.

I insist on this point: The spiritual and mental grasp of the
whole preceded detailed knowledge of each technique and
conditioned its assimilation.

When the demonstrator was in the first place capable of
putting himself in "the state of grace" essential to the sincere
execution of the Kata—almost as in the delivery of a prayer—
the effective presentation of the successive forms was nothing
more than a question of application and of time. When, on
the contrary, he applied himself only to detail without the
determination to identify himself with the whole, then the
form escaped him and the Kàta was no more than a pale and
lustreless reflection without truth or depth.

In other words, in every movement of Kata the judoka (in
France it has become customary to call anybody, no matter
whom, practising Judo a judoka, whereas in Japan the judoka
is at least a 4th Dan and below that grade the student of Judo
is styled a judoshugyosha) inspired by these ancient examples
ought not to seek solely for a pretext to give a good demonstration of detail but also to translate the truth, the continuity
of an entire mental state through a physical representation.

In Judo regarded strictly as a sport the Kata also has its
place.

In Japan the young champions are apt to devote themselves to randori-competition or to shiai, i.e. to competition
only, and this is a great mistake.

That is why the study and practice of the Katas tend to
relegate Judo combat to its true place and why practice of the
Katas equally constitutes a fatiguing and difficult exercise
which enables one to make great progress and affords one an
opportunity to correct and complete the technique. The basic
condition of the sincere and correct study of a Kata is the
respect for form.

"The Form must be very strict because it is the fruit of patient research, extensive experience and is always efficacious. If you strive patiently to practise the Form exactly you will surely and more rapidly attain precision and the best results. A really efficacious style and one agreeable to contemplate is always the fruit of patient quest for basic forms" (Jigoro KANO).

All the Katas constitute in the first place a school of what may be called "progress-Judo", of displacement and "tai-sabaki".

The displacement or "shintai" should often be made in the shape of "Tsugiashi", i.e. the feet graze the mat without being crossed, in succession and not alternately. I shall return to this important point at the beginning of the study of the NAGE-NO-KATA. As regards the "tai-sabaki", this is the management of the body, the feet and the hips, pivoting together, which permits the judoka most easily to attack or resist in the fundamental natural posture, the "shizen-hontai".

Afterwards, unconsciously but surely, with patient assiduous study, theoretical and practical, of these exercises of style, of their spirit and fundamental forms, the judoka will make progress in randori and shiai.

There exist in Japan very many Katas of Judo, Jujutsu and other Martial Arts. The Katas of Judo the best known, the most studied and the most representative of the spirit and style of Judo are the seven Katas explained in this work.

Their objects, their characters and their rhythm are different, as also are the methods of attack and defence of the performers. But the totality of these Katas aims at demonstrating the theory and practice of the various aspects of Judo. That is why, just as each Kata constitutes a whole, the seven Katas in question represent an interdependent and a complementary whole, a synthesis of the great basic principles of Judo under its diverse forms.

The choice of these Katas and for each Kata the diverse techniques has not been empirical but logical. Each Kata is an illustration, a demonstration, but also a strict concatenation or sequence and an instruction founded on the basic principles of Judo—maximum efficiency, total employment of the available energy, mutual aid.

Each displacement has been thought out, each defence is precisely that which best responds to the attack; each hold is at one and the same time necessary and sufficient, as condensed, as complete as the most rigorous demonstration and as the most logical explanation.

The form is guardian of the substance, and the Kata is the perfect illustration of this adage.

Whilst impregnating himself with the spirit, as in the old Jujutsu, the judoka attains the perfect execution of the true and beautiful form, but reciprocally adheres to respect for detail and rediscovers the century-old experience of the old Masters and the general signification of the whole. Moreover do not believe that in such a way we are departing from the domain of sport. In a sport, whatever it may be, understood in a true and broad sense, the respect for form, the solicitude for style, the beauty of gesture have always been characteristic traits of the greatest champions, of those who truly represent the spiritual and educational value of their sport, of those whom the young performer should seek to imitate and if possible to surpass.

What then should be the place of the Katas in the teaching of the judoka? In my opinion, Kata and Randori must be studied (there is a study of Randori) and practised on an equal footing. In Judo there is not an age for Randori and for competition and then later an age for the Kata.

If it is quite normal to leave to the older Masters the illustration and the public demonstration of the Katas, it is equally necessary not to dissociate in the progressive study of Judo these two complementary aspects, Randori and Kata. The Kata will temper the combative ardour of the young performer and will undoubtedly also enable him to discover the reason for certain errors which he commits in competition; will give him the key to the disequilibriums or the entries for which he has vainly searched by means of "butsukari" alone (or "uchi-komi", training by rapid attacks repeated on a partner). Thus the Kata is a valuable source of technical progress.

But intrinsically it is also a difficult exercise, a rigorous discipline, a veritable physical education and it is equally under this aspect that it ought to be considered.

We have seen seasoned champions as well tested after the demonstration of a Kata as after a competition, and this was already at any rate a proof of their sincerity of execution. The accomplishment of a Kata is a physically fatiguing test through the effort exerted, the tension of spirit due to care for perfection of style, to the quest for a true gesture, strict and complete. Consequently even the Kata is also sport.

Another question: among all the Katas and basic exercises, are there some, so to speak, more fundamental than others? Yes, two Katas particularly "open the way", facilitate apprenticeship to Judo, constitute a teaching and a training, furnish a solid technical base and at the same time an excellent preparation for competition.

The matter concerns—which is normal—the two first Katas, the NAGE-NO-KATA, or Kata of Throws, and the KATAME-NO-KATA, or Kata of Judo on the ground. The entirety of these Katas is sometimes called RANDORI-NO-KATA.

I earnestly advise pupils, with the consent and in accordance with the guidance of their teachers, to familiarize themselves relatively soon with these two Katas, i.e. starting from the green or blue belt. They will be surprised at the progress they will make. The other Katas studied in this book are the following:—

The 3rd Kata, GONOSEN-NO-KATA, or Kata of standing counters, specially practised at Waseda University, of which I have been a member;

The 4th Kata, KIME-NO-KATA, or Kata of Defence;

The 5th Kata, ITSUTSU-NO-KATA, or Kata of the Five Principles;

The 6th Kata, JU-NO-KATA, or Kata of Suppleness, sometimes called gentleness;

The 7th Kata, KOSHIKI-NO-KATA, or Ancient Kata.

There are, I repeat, many other Judo Katas. I shall mention only a few which have fallen into disuetude:

The SHOBU-NO-KATA, or Kata of Attack (more literally Contest);

The GO-NO-KATA, or Kata of Force or of blows, more characteristic of KARATE-DO (the technique of the Atemis).

At the Kodokan they still study the SEIRYOKU-ZENYO-KOKUMIN-TAIIKU-NO-KATA, or Kata of Physical Training, as also two derived from the KIME-NO-KATA, a Kata of Defence for Women and another a little different for Men.

In this work I propose before the study of each Kata to give a brief analysis designed to elucidate its essential characteristics: history, object, spirit, rhythm. I shall also point out, when the opportunity offers, the slight differences introduced, according to the Schools, in the execution of certain movements.

I trust that this book may serve all French judokas by helping them to understand, practise and love the Katas which constitute, as my Master Jigoro KANO has very justly said, "the essence and the beauty of Judo", and the best means of finding the "way".

"Study the Katas and you will arrive at the truth and the beauty of Judo".

PREFATORY NOTE

THE presentation of this work is very like the preceding one: "My Method of Self-Defence". A Figure Number against each movement indicates its respective drawing.

The various phases of the movements are studied by paragraphs.

TORI, he who executes the hold, is always dark and wears a black belt; UKE, he who suffers the hold, is always light with a shaded belt.

Each "time" marking the Kata forms the object of a drawing. The drawings are numbered to facilitate general comprehension and study of the movement. The references in the text to the drawings are made with their numbers indicated in parentheses.

The study of the Katas is reserved for judokas already sufficiently experienced and possessing at least two years' practice. Also on the drawings some arrows mark only the essential displacements, since all the holds are supposed to be known.

For each movement the Japanese name is given with the French (English: *Translator's Note*) translation, as also the number corresponding to the French nomenclature of the Kawaishi Method.

The references to the movements of Judo or of Self-Defence of the two preceding works are made as follows: (*Judo*, page ..., *Self-Defence*, page ...).

TRANSLATOR'S PREFACE

"The cry is 'Still They Come!' " And from the same source
—a veritable Judo cornucopia! The debt which the non-
Japanese Judo world already owes to Mikonosuke Kawaishi
Shihan, 7th Dan, for his two earlier books entitled respectively
My Method of Judo and *My Method of Self-Defence*, both of
which I have been privileged to translate from the original
French into English, has now been increased by the present
no less important work entitled *The Complete 7 Katas of Judo*.
And now again I have been charged with the responsible
but grateful task of furnishing English readers with an English
version of this latest contribution to the ever-growing biblio-
graphy of Judo. Last but by no means least!

So far as I know there is no other non-Japanese work available containing under one cover an authoritative exposition
of the seven fundamental Katas of Judo, viz., NAGE-NO-
KATA, KATAME-NO-KATA, GONOSEN-NO-KATA, KIME-NO-
KATA, ITSUTSU-NO-KATA, JU-NO-KATA, and KOSHIKI-
NO-KATA. Such being the case I make bold to say that
M. Kawaishi's *The Complete 7 Katas of Judo* really does
appear upon the scene in time "to fill a long-felt want".
I may even go farther and add that, in my opinion,
no aspiring judoka can afford to omit this book from his list
of indispensable works of reference on the art. Opinions may
and doubtless do differ on the varying degrees of *practical*
value possessed by these seven Katas in the Judo curriculum.
And iconoclasts are not wanting who question more particularly the need for the Itsutsu-no-Kata (Kata of the Five
Principles) and perhaps the Ju-no-Kata (Kata of Suppleness
or Gentleness) in the empirical equipment of the modern
non-Japanese yudansha. Admittedly among the less devout
"disciples" (montei) names such as "principle of concentration of energy", "principle of reaction and of non-resistance",
"principle of flux and reflux", "principle of the void or of
inertia", and "principle of centripetal and centrifugal force"
are apt to provoke a somewhat furtive smile and elevated
eyebrows. Yet the fact remains that most higher-ranking
Japanese yudansha are competent to demonstrate all seven
of these Katas and that the illustrious founder of the art of
Judo, the late Jigoro Kano himself, always insisted upon the
necessity for knowledge of the Katas among Judo graduates.

Nor can the fact be gainsaid that to hard training in the

Katas must be attributed the greater suppleness of foot, knee, hip and loin, more especially, which generally differentiates Japanese from western judoka and which in its turn is contributory to the average superiority of Japanese judoka over our western product. And in this context serious study of M. Kawaishi's present work should suffice to convince even the most sceptical that the tremendous physical and even "spiritual" demands made upon the human organism by sustained practice of the Katas, combined with their public demonstration, can hardly fail to redound to the judoka's advantage in both Randori and Shiai.

The bodily movements called for by the Katas are so multifarious that they may be said to anticipate most of the contingencies likely to arise on the mat beyond the "axis of the Katas" themselves. The yudansha skilled in the Katas can usually be recognized by the polish, elegance and grace, the "reflex" quality of his throws and counters in Randori and Shiai. And unless the judoka has mastered at least the Nage-no-Kata, Gonosen-no-Kata and Kime-no-Kata, and perhaps the truly impressive Koshiki-no-Kata, his breakfalls are likely to fall short of perfection!

As in the case of my translations of M. Kawaishi's previous works the principal latitude I have permitted myself in the present version has been the standardization of the English renderings of the author's French names of the approved techniques more or less in conformity with accepted usage at The Budokwai and in affiliated clubs in this country. Otherwise his frequent inclusion of these references to the French text of his *My Method of Judo* when describing a relevant method in the Kata would be meaningless to English readers. A further simplification which seemed advisable has been the conversion into plain English of sundry anatomical expressions to which French writers on Judo are unduly prone, such as "the cubital edge" and "the radial edge" of the arm, "the thenar eminence" and "the hypothenar eminence" of the hand, "in supination", "in pronation", &c., &c. Not every judoka can be expected to have at his elbow a textbook on physiology and anatomy for the purpose of ascertaining the meaning of these abstruse terms. Clarity is a far too important desideratum to admit of these lapses into physiological preciosity!

For a more comprehensive survey of the nature, scope and purpose of the Katas in the Judo curriculum I cannot do better than refer the reader to M. Kawaishi's own Foreword.

E. J. H.

THE COMPLETE 7 KATAS OF JUDO

I

FIRST KATA
OR
NAGE-NO-KATA
(Kata of Throws)

The NAGE-NO-KATA, or Kata of the Throws, the First Part of the RANDORI-NO-KATA, or Forms of Free Exercise, was created by the late Professor Jigoro KANO, who has definitively fixed therein the form and the spirit.

Its exemplary execution represents the ideal application of the theoretical rules of the throws.

It constitutes the basis of the study of the principles of attack and defence of standing Judo (NAGE-WAZA), of the displacements (SHINTAI), and of the movements of the body (TAI-SABAKI).

It is in the entire sense of the term the First Kata of Judo, the Kata-type, the Kata-key.

Tradition requires that the demonstration of the First Kata should usher in all Judo displays and competitions in order to put contestants and spectators in touch with the environment of Judo.

It is composed of 15 throws grouped in 5 Series of 3 movements each, as indicated in the following Table:

FIRST KATA

(15 *movements*)

1st Series—Hand Techniques: TE-WAZA

2nd Arm Throw: UKI-OTOSHI (Floating Drop)

1st Shoulder Throw: KATA-SEOI (Shoulder Throw from one side only)

3rd Shoulder Throw: KATA-GURUMA (Shoulder Wheel)

2nd Series—Hip and Loin Techniques: KOSHI-WAZA

1st Hip Throw: UKI-GOSHI (Floating Loin)

5th Hip Throw: HARAI-GOSHI (Sweeping Loin Throw)

8th Hip Throw: TSURI-KOMI-GOSHI (Drawing Hip or Loin Throw)

3rd Series—Leg and Foot Techniques: ASHI-WAZA

7th Leg Throw: OKURI-ASHI-BARAI (Sweeping Ankle Throw)

11th Leg Throw: SASAE-TSURI-KOMI-ASHI (Propping Drawing Ankle Throw)

10th Hip Throw: (As classified by M. Kawaishi, but according to The Kodokan a Leg Throw): UCHI-MATA (Inner Thigh Throw)

4th Series—Techniques of Sutemi on the Back: MA-SUTEMI-WAZA

1st Sutemi (or Sacrifice Throw): TOMOE-NAGE (Stomach Throw or Throwing in a Circle)

12th Sutemi: URA-NAGE (Rear Throw)

7th Sutemi: SUMI-GAESHI (Corner Throw)

5th Series—Techniques of Sutemi on the Side: YOKO-SUTEMI-WAZA

5th Sutemi: YOKO-GAKE (Lateral Hook)

13th Sutemi: YOKO-GURUMA (Lateral Wheel)

8th Sutemi: UKI-WAZA (Floating Throw)

1st KATA—PRELIMINARIES

The SALUTATION "kamiza" (literally "upper seat") to the Masters and the spectators should be made at the same time by Tori and Uke before and after the demonstration of each Kata.

The place of honour where the Masters are seated is called the "Joseki".

In France for all the Katas, except for the 7th, in relation to the "Joseki", Tori stands to the right and Uke to the left to salute, at least nine feet in front and about 15 feet one from the other.

In Japan it is the same for the 1st, 2nd, 3rd, 4th and 6th Katas, but the reverse for the 5th and 7th Katas.

At the beginning of the 1st Kata Tori and Uke are therefore facing each other, side face to the "Joseki", separated by 12 or 15 feet in the fundamental natural posture, or Shizen-hontai (1).

They pivot together at an angle of about 30 degrees, Tori to the left and Uke to the right, to salute standing the "Joseki" (2).

The salutation must not be perfunctory and artificial but addressed in a characteristic manner to the Master in whose honour the Kata is being executed, to whom it is "dedicated", usually the expert most elevated in grade or the President of the assemblage.

Sometimes after the traditional salutation to the "Joseki" at great public demonstrations which are given on a raised platform, Tori and Uke symmetrically make another salutation in the direction opposite to the "Joseki" to show that they dedicate the Kata which they are going to execute to the spectators as a whole.

The STANDING SALUTATION must convey the respect of the demonstrators for the Masters and for the spectators, as well as for the forms of Judo which they are going to execute. This should be an exemplary salutation. Fig. 1.

Tori and Uke join their heels without stiffness and without abruptness, ceremoniously but simply and without affectation, the upper part of the body inclined forward, the hands, palms flat and fingers joined, allowed to slide along the thighs, the nape of the neck remaining in the line of the shoulders and the eyes starting from those of the recipient of the salutation to descend as far as his feet, then ascend to his face, as the bust is straightened when the salutation is completed.

The KNEELING SALUTATION. Fig. 1 (3 to 7).

TORI and UKE again face each other in order to execute the kneeling salutation.

They lower themselves together on to their heels, hands sliding along their thighs to the knees, then without displacing

Fig. I

their feet they place their knees on the ground, first the right, then the left.

They then salute each other kneeling, in the fundamental salutation of Judo, as follows: The knees separated from each other by about 10 inches (the distance approximately represented by two fists placed side by side between the knees) the hips resting on the heels, the palms of the hands flat on the ground on either side of the knees, fingers joined with the end of the fingers pointed inwards, the bust and the head in the same line bending towards the ground rather slowly and without stiffness. The toes remain bent and not extended against the mat as for the position of repose or for the ceremonial salutation which should include one "time" more necessary to extend and then to bend back the toes.

This flexion of the toes is explained by the fact that the 1st Kata is a Randori-No-Kata and that the action begins immediately after the salutation. This salutation does not represent a pause and the feet remain in support bent on the ground and not extended in a position of relaxation.

The salutation having been effected TORI and UKE stand up again while marking the same "times" as for kneeling, but in the reverse direction, i.e. first lifting the left knee, then the right.

DISPLACEMENT, Shintai. This has already been mentioned in the Preface. The feet of TORI and UKE must always lightly brush the mat and must never be crossed. Fig. 1 (8).

TORI and UKE should never adjust their judogi in the course of the execution of a Series. At the end of each Series they return to their initial place of salutation, face each other and put their jacket in order by pulling from each side on the points of the lapels, Fig. 1 (9), the left above the right (for female performers it is the reverse).

In Japan, the preliminaries of the 1st Kata having been accomplished as they have just been described, TORI and UKE take a step forward with the left foot, mark a pause in the natural posture, then they approach each other always starting from the left foot and changing position from the fundamental manner until there is only about a distance of three feet between them.

In France, in the current execution of the 1st Kata, after the salutation, UKE standing facing TORI does not move and awaits UKE's approach towards him. In demonstration it is better to operate according to the Japanese rite.

1st KATA—1st Series

1.—UKI-OTOSHI (Floating Drop) *Fig.* 2
2nd Arm Throw (*Judo*, page 76)

The axis of displacement of the 1st Kata, before the "Joseki", can be diagrammatized by two lines, two "rails" defined by

Tori's left foot and Uke's right foot on the one hand, and on the other by Tori's right foot and Uke's left foot for the distance to go—throw to the right—vice versa for the return distance—throw to the left.

The throws always take place either from the empty space

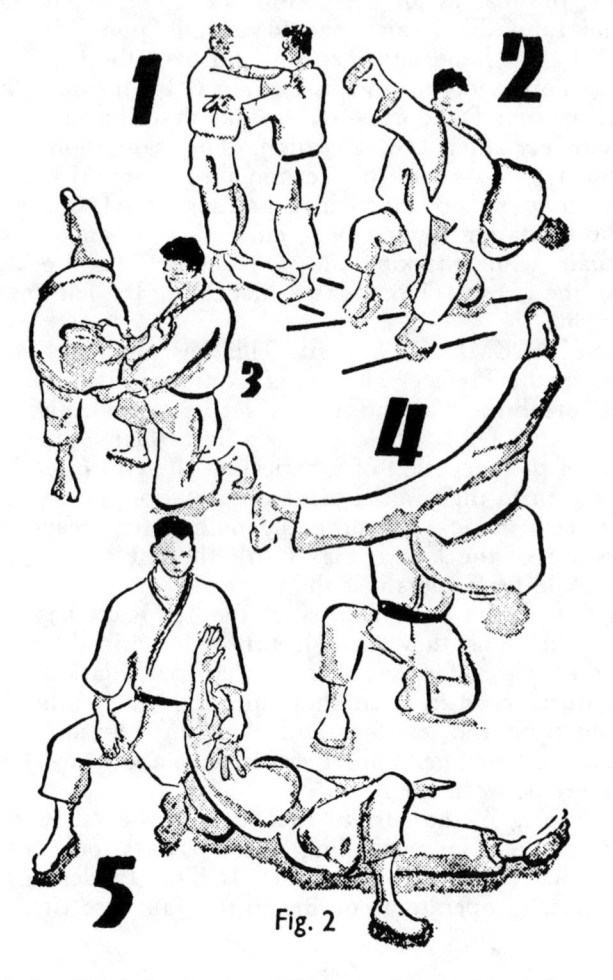

Fig. 2

created by Tori in front of Uke in the axis of these rails, Tori placing himself on the side, or else from the fact that Tori, inside the rails in question, places himself so as to make Uke rest and swing on him.

Tori comes in front of Uke halfway, i.e. in a position to seize the judogi, his arms not completely stretched. He simultaneously and not too quickly raises his arms and takes hold of UKE's judogi in the fundamental grip, "kumi-kata", of Judo, his left hand on UKE's right sleeve and his right hand on UKE's left lapel (*Judo*, page 19). UKE makes the same movement at the same time: he waits for TORI to begin to raise his arms and must at the same time ensure his hand holds.

As soon as this reciprocal contact is acquired, without the slightest pause UKE advances his right foot while TORI withdraws his left foot (1) a first time, then a second time, accentuating UKE's right-front disequilibrium. TORI and UKE have therefore successively taken two steps without crossing their feet (displacement tsugiashi).

At the third step TORI pivots a quarter turn to the left on his right foot and places his left knee on the ground on an axis of displacement of his right foot. The toes of his left foot should remain bent (2 and 3). UKE is forcibly unbalanced forward at the moment of beginning his third step (2 and 3). He does a "kata-fall" forward around the axis represented by his right forearm and TORI's left forearm (4) and falls in the axis of displacement to the left of TORI's left knee. UKE's legs must not be crossed (5).

TORI remains with the upper part of his body straight in the exemplary position of KATAME-NO-KATA, holding UKE in the course of his fall.

TORI and UKE stand up again face to face in the axis of displacement, but this time TORI to the left and UKE to the right of the "Joseki", and now change their grip to the style of the left natural posture in which TORI and UKE respectively grasp their opponent's right lapel with the left hand and his left sleeve with the right hand.

TORI throws UKE this time by placing his right knee on the ground after having effected the displacements symmetrically to the preceding ones.

TORI and UKE rise to their feet and return to the same respective positions as at the start of the Kata.

Remark: There will be no further need to describe in detail the execution of the other throws to the left since, subject to the relevant changes of hold and stance, the execution of these movements is on all fours with their execution as described for the fundamental throws to the right.

In Japan the execution is sometimes a little different; it is UKE who advances on TORI and the latter who recedes before the pushing, whereas in France the initiative comes from TORI who effects a movement of traction on UKE's sleeve. In ceremonial demonstrations it is preferable that TORI and UKE should rejoin each other in the centre of the mat.

1st KATA—1st Series

2.—KATA-SEOI (Shoulder Throw from one side)
Fig. 3
1st Shoulder Throw (*Judo*, page 67)

Fig. 3

TORI has just thrown UKE with the Uki-Otoshi to the left. He has lifted his right knee from the ground while UKE has regained his feet. Both are face to face in the initial position before contact, separated by about six feet.

UKE takes a big step forward with his left foot at the

moment when TORI is moving towards him. UKE has brought his right arm from behind, the fist clenched, to gain the impetus necessary to strike the crown of TORI's skull with the lower part of his fist (the hypothenar eminence or muscles accupying the medial side of the little finger). The impetus of UKE's body resembles that of a weight-putter (1).

TORI advances his right foot in front of the right foot of UKE who has made a second step and rests on his right leg just before striking TORI with his lowered fist (2 and 3).

At the same time TORI has lifted his left arm and the cubital or little-finger edge of his wrist directed upwards blocks the wrist of UKE who is beginning the descending movement (2 and 3).

TORI then pivots on his right foot towards his left and places his left foot on the same transversal line (in relation to the general axis of displacement UKE-TORI) as his right foot.

TORI's right arm is placed under UKE's right armpit and TORI takes advantage of the forward impetus of UKE to throw him as described in the same author's work on *Judo*, pages 67-68 (4).

UKE should execute a pretty kata-fall over TORI's shoulders, taking support at the start of the throw with his left hand resting on TORI's left hip and stretching his legs well (5 and 6). The throw and fall must be perfectly natural and true.

1st KATA—1st Series

3.—KATA-GURUMA (Shoulder Wheel) *Fig.* 4
3rd Shoulder Throw (*Judo*, page 69)

TORI and UKE take hold of each other in the right natural posture, i.e. right hand gripping opponent's left lapel and left hand his right sleeve (1).

At the moment when they take the first step TORI's left hand winds round over UKE's arm, i.e. it lets go its hold on the external surface of UKE's right sleeve to take hold of the inner surface of the biceps (2). This change of hold, as also those which we shall subsequently see, must be effected in the course of the first step. In Japan it is sometimes accomplished during the second step. The hold with UKE's right hand on TORI's judogi ought not therefore to be too tight so as to offer resistance to the semi-circular movement of TORI's left forearm.

In the course of the third step TORI lowers himself and taking advantage of UKE's advance throws him with the 3rd fundamental Shoulder Throw described in the same author's

Judo, pages 69-70. The illustration depicts this action clearly enough. Thus TORI's right hand, which has relinquished its grip of UKE's left lapel, takes a firm hold of UKE's right thigh from behind and swings him athwart TORI's shoulders behind TORI's neck (3 to 6).

Fig. 4

TORI must remain with his bust straight (4).

His feet are kept separated during the entire throw; or if necessary TORI may bring his left foot against his right to accentuate the turning movement, wheel-like, of the throw as a whole.

Throw symmetrical to the left which terminates the 1st Series.

1st KATA—2nd Series

1.—UKI-GOSHI (Floating Loin) *Fig.* 5
1st Hip Throw (*Judo*, page 45)

Fig. 5

TORI and UKE have readjusted their judogis. They breathe deeply before beginning the 2nd Series. The pause should last only a few seconds.

TORI moves towards UKE always in the fundamental displacement, normal step but the feet lightly brushing against the mat.

When TORI reaches about six feet from UKE the latter

attacks as for the 2nd movement of the 1st Series (1). We have already seen that in Japan the approach of TORI and UKE is sometimes simultaneous.

TORI pivots towards his right on his right foot and places his left foot, toes turned in the direction of the rotation, in front of UKE's left foot at the moment when UKE takes his second step with his right foot for attack and is lowering his right arm (2).

Taking support on his left foot TORI brings his right foot on the same transversal line (3).

His left arm encircles UKE's waist passing under his right arm (2).

TORI's right hand seizes the inner surface of UKE's left sleeve (3). TORI throws UKE with 1st fundamental Loin Throw to the left (Uki-Goshi). TORI's feet are inside those of UKE (4 and 5).

Symmetrical execution to the right, i.e. on UKE's attack with his left hand.

Remark: For this throw TORI can also effect a "rotative entry", advance his right foot sufficiently far on the line of UKE's right foot, then without crossing his feet, from close to pivot to the right on the toes of his right foot so as to place his left foot in front of and a little to the inside of that of UKE.

1st KATA—2nd Series

2.—HARAI-GOSHI (Sweeping Loin) *Fig.* 6
5th Loin Throw (*Judo*, page 49)

Customary hold in the right natural posture and first step (1).

In the course of the first step TORI slips his right hand under UKE's left armpit and supports his palm against UKE's left shoulder-blade (1 and 2).

TORI takes his third step and pivots backwards to the left on his left foot to effect "change of rail", i.e. he places himself on the axis of the left foot of UKE and sufficiently in front of him.

TORI, with his left wrist hook-wise, continues his movement of traction forward and upwards on UKE's right arm (3).

TORI then throws UKE with the fundamental 5th Loin Throw or HARAI-GOSHI (4 and 5). The illustration shows that TORI with his right leg powerfully sweeps UKE's right leg obliquely almost parallel to the line of UKE's feet. This sweeping action is made from the hip and with the entire length of the thigh.

Symmetrical execution then ensues to the left with the necessary readjustments.

Fig. 6

1st KATA—2nd Series

3.—TSURI-KOMI-GOSHI (Drawing Hip or Loin Throw)

Fig. 7

8th Loin Throw (*Judo*, page 54)

The customary hold in the right natural posture (1) and in the course of the first step TORI's right hand ascends the length of UKE's left lapel to seize his collar behind the nape (2).

TORI's left foot effects the "change of rail" in the course of the third step as in the preceding throw.

When UKE advances his right foot to end his third step TORI places his right foot in front of UKE's right foot. TORI's

Fig. 7

feet are thus inside those of UKE in the fundamental position.

TORI, taking advantage of UKE's advance, essays to make him swing over the top of his right hip, but by scarcely flexing his knees (3).

UKE resists from the abdomen but without bending backwards.

Tori then cleanly flexes his legs, knees separated, and throws Uke (4 and 5) with the Tsuri-Komi-Goshi, i.e. his right hand remains on Uke's neck and does not take hold of his left sleeve as in the Sode-Tsuri-Komi-Goshi.

Remark: In this throw, as in the preceding one, Tori often has a tendency at the beginning of the study of the 1st Kata to take a third step which is not sufficiently marked. To enable him to find the true distance it is better for him to take too big rather than too small a step and to exaggerate the movement, as in the initial study of no matter what Judo technique.

1st KATA—3rd Series

1.—OKURI-ASHI-BARAI (Sweeping Ankle Throw)
Fig. 8
7th Leg Throw (*Judo*, page 33)

Pause necessary for readjustment of judogi.

Tori walks up to Uke who awaits him without stirring. At the moment when Tori reaches about three feet from Uke, Uke pivots a quarter turn to the right, slightly advances his left foot and withdraws his right foot in such wise as to bring it on the axis of his left foot. Tori at the same time effects the complementary symmetrical movement which brings him in front of Uke, both feet side by side on the axis of his left foot which was that of Uke's right foot and which Uke has just quit.

As soon as Tori and Uke are face to face, side face in relation to the axis of displacement, Tori turning his back to the "Joseki" and Uke facing it, both hold each other in the right natural posture which the author calls "fundamental guard", and the displacement begins. In Japan this displacement is sometimes transversal without Tori and Uke pivoting a quarter turn.

The displacement is made with lateral Tsugiashi. Tori advances his right foot with a fairly big step to the right slowly and lightly grazing the mat as he pulls Uke towards his right. Uke takes the same step with his left foot to the left. The second step, similar but quicker and more "lifted" follows accompanied by a hook-wise more marked upward movement with Tori's wrists.

Third step still quicker and movement more accentuated. During this third step Tori sweeps laterally from left to right with his left foot UKE's right ankle in the direction of his displacement and throws him with the 7th fundamental leg throw (OKURI-ASHI-BARAI) explained in the same author's *Judo*, pages 33-34. The impact of TORI's left foot against

Fig. 8

UKE's right ankle occurs at the moment when UKE raises his right foot to rejoin his left foot (3, 4 and 5).

Remark: TORI ought not to pretend but effect the movement seriously. The sweep, the contact of the sole of his foot with UKE's ankle must be real and energetic. The primary quality of a Kata is its sincerity, its truth.

1st KATA—3rd Series

2.—SASAE-TSURI-KOMI-ASHI (Propping Drawing Ankle Throw) *Fig.* 9
11th Leg Throw (*Judo,* page 38)

Fig. 9

Right natural posture.

When TORI takes his third step he does not interrupt the withdrawal of his right foot effected in the second step; on the contrary he prolongs it in the following manner: His right heel describes flush with the mat an arc behind towards the right at about a foot to the right of the axis of displacement, otherwise "outside the rails" and at about a foot behind the transversal line marking the second step, passed as it were by his right foot.

At the same time TORI continues to exercise with his left wrist a vigorous traction forward and upward on UKE's right arm in the direction of its displacement. TORI lifts his left leg and with the sole of the foot blocks UKE's right tibia in the act of ending his forward step. UKE's left foot is still behind and has not begun the third step which would make it rejoin his right foot (1).

TORI thus throws UKE with the 11th fundamental leg throw, or SASAE-TSURI-KOMI-ASHI. UKE does a kata-fall in the axis of displacement (2). The entire throw resembles in its displacement and principle the 1st of the 1st Series (UKI-OTOSHI) since here also TORI "makes a vacuum" in front of UKE.

1st KATA—3rd Series

3.—UCHI-MATA (Inner Thigh) *Fig.* 10
10th Hip Throw (*Judo*, page 56)

TORI and UKE in the right natural posture, i.e. TORI's right hand slides along UKE's left lapel to seize it a little higher than the normal hold against his chin below the ear (1).

TORI with his right hand pulls UKE's left lapel towards his right back and above. At the same time he advances his left foot a half step towards his left front so that being un-balanced UKE makes the corresponding displacement sym-metrically opposite. The feet of UKE and TORI are then placed respectively on both sides of the axis of displacement of the Kata.

The second step of TORI and UKE is similar to the first; the movement of rotation always proceeds in the direction of the hands of a watch.

TORI's third step is more marked than the preceding ones, but his left supporting foot is placed clearly inside the circle of general rotation of the movement (3 and 4).

The displacement of UKE's feet in the course of the two first times are represented in diagram 2.

TORI does not finish his third step in the sense that he largely advances his left foot (diagram 3) but when he has his legs separated, without waiting until his right foot rejoins his left, supporting himself on his left foot, as has just been indicated, he thrusts his right leg between UKE's legs in such wise that the external posterior surface of his thigh sweeps the inner surface of UKE's left thigh (5).

UKE is thrown with the 10th fundamental Hip Throw (6). Coincident with this sweep TORI leans forward so that his body and right leg are in a direct line, the lowest portion of

Fig. 10

the rocker being his head. TORI's arms draw UKE forward as much as possible and preserve contact between his abdomen, his right hip and his chest on the one hand and TORI's right flank on the other, from the thigh to the shoulder. UKE is extended face downwards on this axis round which he pivots and falls.

As for all the other movements execution follows exactly symmetrical to the left. This ends the 3rd Series.

(*Translator's Note:* Although in conformity with his own classification our author calls the Uchi-Mata a hip throw

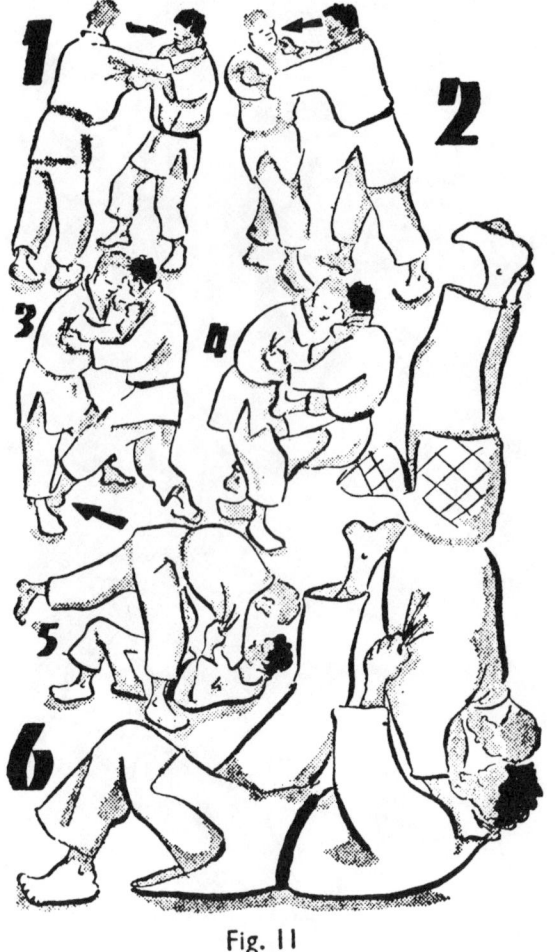

Fig. II

(Koshiwaza), for the purpose of the Kodokan-Nage-no-Kata it is regarded as a Leg Throw (Ashiwaza). It is therefore advisable that the reader should note this discrepancy when studying this Series. Opinions are known to differ in the Judo world on the just apportionment of the roles of leg and hip in this particular technique, but here is no place for the obtrusion of a polemic on the subject.)

1st KATA—4th Series

1.—TOMOE-NAGE (Throw in Circle or Stomach Throw)
Fig. 11
1st SUTEMI (*Judo*, page 87)

TORI approaches UKE.

At the moment when TORI is close to him UKE seizes him in the right natural posture and vigorously pushes him backwards several times (1).

TORI reacts and in his turn pushes UKE until he returns to his original position (2).

UKE then opposes very strong resistance to TORI's pushing and is going once more to make him retreat. UKE has blocked TORI's advance with his stomach and separated legs.

TORI then places his left foot, heel trailing on the ground, between UKE's feet and far behind his heels (3).

Then he drops to the ground and places the sole of his right foot, toes bent, against UKE's abdomen below the navel (4).

UKE advances his right leg to the outside of TORI's left flank at the level of the belt (5).

He is thrown with the 1st Sutemi (TOMOE-NAGE) and executes a forward fall (6).

Remark: In Japan it is TORI who begins to push UKE backwards. Then at the start of the fall TORI's left hand relinquishes its grip on UKE's right sleeve to seize his right lapel. When pupils begin to study this movement it is well that they should accustom themselves to making together three rapid steps, pushing forward and then back in order not to commit a foot fault at the outset of the throw.

1st KATA—4th Series

2.—URA-NAGE (Rear Throw) *Fig.* 12
12th SUTEMI (*Judo*, page 98)

TORI advances towards UKE. When he is about six feet from him UKE attacks him as in the 2nd Movement 1st Series (KATA-SEOI) or the 1st Movement of the second (Uki-Goshi) (2).

TORI bends forward with his head lowered to dodge the blow. He places his right foot in front of UKE's right foot (2), then his left foot a little behind UKE's right heel (3) so as to have both feet appreciably on the axis of displacement of UKE's right foot. TORI may also directly place his left foot on the outside and a little behind UKE's right foot.

Tori's head rests in front of Uke and is pressed against his right pectoral. Tori's right arm holds Uke's abdomen, the hand placed a little below the thorax, while his left arm encompasses Uke's waist behind at the level of his belt and as far back as his left loin. His knees are bent and carrying

Fig. 12

the weight of both bodies on his heels, above all the right which must not stir. He hurls himself backwards in the axis of Uke's advance, in accordance with the fundamental execution of the Ura-Nage (*Judo*, page 93) (4).

Uke does a forward fall somewhat obliquely, which he blocks on the ground where he lies extended by the throw and therefore prevented from rolling forward and regaining his feet (5 and 6).

1st KATA—4th Series

3.—SUMI-GAESHI (Corner Throw) *Fig.* 13
7th Sᴜᴛᴇᴍɪ (*Judo*, page 93)

Fig. 13

Tᴏʀɪ approaches to halfway from Uᴋᴇ. Simultaneously, he separates his feet widely (about 32 inches to a foot), knees bent at a right-angle above his feet, thus in the self-defensive posture, or jigotai. Their right hands pass under each other's left armpits and are placed, the palm flat, on the left shoulder-blades. Their left hands pull on their right sleeves. Their heads rest with their cheeks supported on each other's shoulder (1).

TORI recedes a small step with his left foot and UKE follows the movement with his right foot (2).

TORI falls back another step with his right foot and UKE follows with his left foot (3). TORI and UKE should trail their feet above all on the extreme edges which do not leave

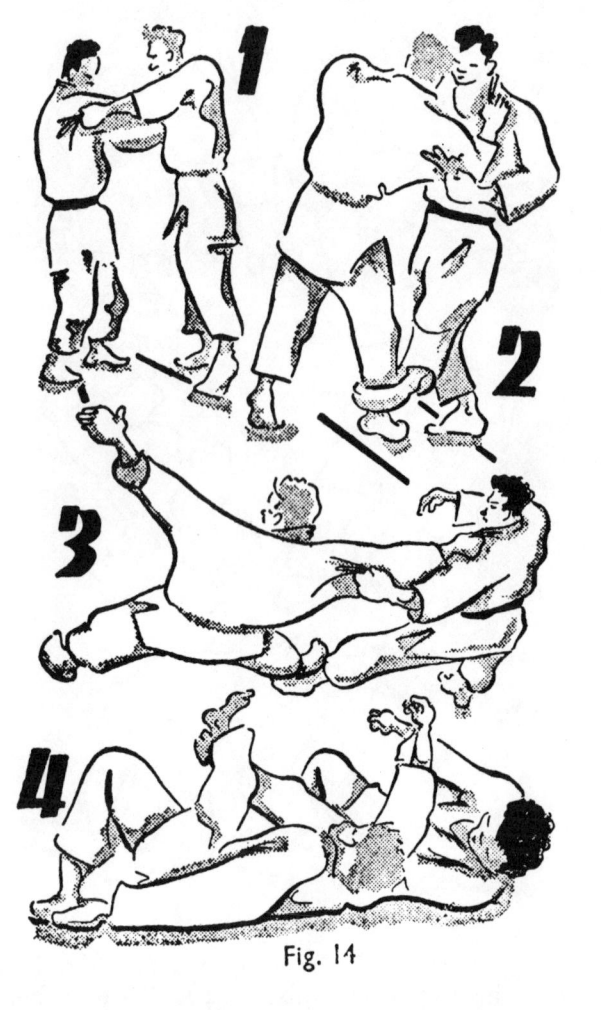

Fig. 14

the mat, like plantigrades, and literally "roll" on their hips. Their steps are semi-circular displacements from one side to another.

TORI then advances his left foot far between the feet of UKE who at this moment disengages his right arm until then wedged under TORI's left armpit (4).

Tori falls on to his back and his right instep lifts Uke's left knee and thigh according to the fundamental execution of the 7th Sutemi except that Tori's left leg is between Uke's legs (5).

Uke executes a rolling frontal fall and comes to his feet behind Tori.

Remark: In Japan the execution of this movement is sometimes a little different. Tori first retracts his right foot, next his left, and then directly throws Uke.

1st KATA—5th Series

1.—YOKO-GAKE (Lateral Hook) *Fig.* 14
5th Sutemi (*Judo*, page 91)

Tori and Uke engage each other in the right natural posture. Tori falls back three successive steps always in the fundamental displacement of Kata, the Tsugiashi, or following foot. At each step with a combined movement of the wrists he forces Uke to shift his position obliquely inclined on his right side (1).

Tori and Uke take their third step but at the precise moment when Uke is going to end it, his back turned completely to the "Joseki", his left foot on the ground, his right foot touching the mat only with his toes (2),—

Tori throws Uke with the 5th fundamental Sutemi (3), Yoko-Gake, in which he vigorously pushes with his left foot the back of Uke's right leg just above the ankle, while with his left hand, which holds Uke's right arm as high as possible, he pulls Uke sideways to Uke's right back. Both fall on to their backs almost side by side, but Uke's fall is quite severe (4).

As in all the other movements the throw is then demonstrated to the left.

1st KATA—5th Series

2.—YOKO-GURUMA (Lateral Wheel) *Fig.* 15
13th Sutemi (*Judo*, page 99)

Exactly the same start as for the 2nd Movement of the 4th Series, the 12th Sutemi, Ura-Nage (1).

The same rotative dodging by Tori with equally the

alternative of either pivoting on his right foot (2) or advancing direct his left foot.

The same blockage, both TORI's legs on both sides of UKE's right foot on his axis of displacement (3).

But at this moment UKE wants to avoid being thrown with

Fig. 15

the URA-NAGE and for this purpose bends forward. TORI's arms immediately encompass UKE as in the Ura-Nage, but are slightly more bent, his right hand on UKE's abdominals, his left on UKE's dorsal vertebrae and therefore less towards UKE's left hip. TORI throws UKE obliquely clearly beyond the axis of displacement.

UKE performs a rolling fall more lateral than clear forward

which separates him from the axis of displacement by an angle of about 60 degrees (5 and 6).

He gets up, does not return to the axis of displacement, but on the contrary makes his attack to the left, approximately from the point of his fall so that when TORI has thrown him symmetrically to the left UKE will be standing at his starting point on the axis of displacement, but with his back to it, since he will end his lateral fall left front.

1st KATA—5th Series

3.—UKI-WAZA (Floating Throw) *Fig.* 16
8th SUTEMI (*Judo*, page 94)

The same hold and the same displacement for the first two steps of TORI and UKE as for the 3rd throw of the 4th Series, the 7th SUTEMI, SUMI-GAESHI (1).

At the third step TORI slips his left leg widely opened and stretched, heel on the mat, at a right-angle, transversely towards his own left, at the same time as his wrists have lifted UKE on his tiptoes unbalanced forward (2).

TORI then lets himself fall on to his left side and throws UKE above his left shoulder (3).

TORI is placed transversely in relation to the axis of displacement and UKE swings and makes a lateral fall high over TORI's left leg which is extended with its outer surface on the ground (4). UKE's fall is effected in the axis of displacement.

The throw is then executed to the left and this ends the 1st KATA. TORI returns to his initial position. He and UKE adjust their judogi. Both are then in the fundamental natural posture, or Shizenhontai, and are facing each other. They salute each other kneeling exactly as at the beginning of the Kata, rise together and standing salute the "Joseki".

───────────

A Kata, as we have said, is a thorough selection of forms and fundamental techniques.

In the course of this study of the 1st KATA we have already been able to state, e.g. with the "digest" of standing Judo, that it does not concern only throws properly speaking, which constitute its backbone, but also different holds to right and left, with their changes, displacements, entries and falls, then the whole of the movements: tsukuri, kake and ukemi.

We have also seen that some variants of interpretation are possible for certain movements of the 1st KATA, e.g. for the preparatory displacements of TORI and UKE, or again for the "entries".

We therefore emphasize that TORI and UKE must always respect the general spirit of the Kata in its fundamental

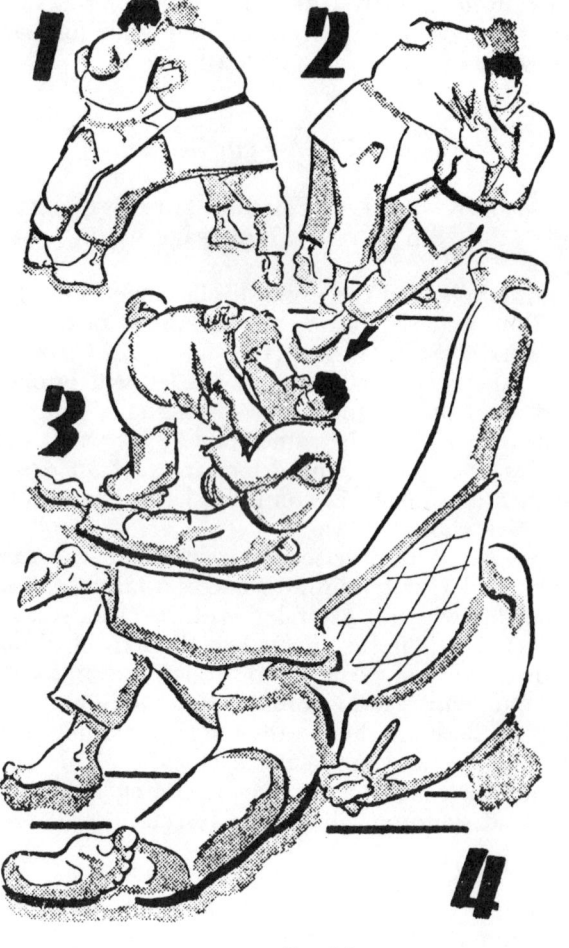

Fig. 16

execution, its continuity and its cohesion, i.e. that TORI should always "go to meet" UKE in the same way and should always operate in an exactly symmetrical manner to right and left, particularly to execute the "entry" for the throw.

It is a mistake to execute an "entry" direct from one side and rotative from the other.

II

SECOND KATA
OR
KATAME-NO-KATA
(Kata on the Ground)

The KATAME-NO-KATA, or Kata of Control, constitutes the second part of the RANDORI-NO-KATA. It was created and its definitive form fixed by the late Professor Jigoro KANO. It determines the theoretical and practical study of the attacks and defences of Judo on the ground. It is classified in three series:

Immobilizations (OSAE-WAZA)

Strangulations (SHIME-WAZA)

Dislocations (KANSETSU-WAZA)

Each series comprises 5 fundamental movements, as indicated in the table on the two following pages.

Remark: The techniques of Judo on the ground are often grouped under the generic appellation of NE-WAZA. This is a mistake because the NE-WAZA is applied only in the recumbent or squatting position, whereas the KATAME-WAZA includes indiscriminately all the techniques of control, whatever may be the initial and final positions in which they are applied.

SECOND KATA
(15 Movements)

1st Series—*Immobilizations: OSAE-WAZA*
- 1st Immobilization: KESA-GATAME (Scarf Hold)
- 2nd Immobilization: KATA-GATAME (Shoulder Lock)
- 3rd Immobilization: KAMI-SHIHO-GATAME) (Locking of the Upper Four Quarters)
- 6th Immobilization: YOKO-SHIHO-GATAME (Lateral Locking of the Four Quarters)
- 4th Immobilization: KUZURE-KAMI-SHIHO-GATAME (Broken Locking of the Upper Four Quarters)

2nd Series—*Strangulations: SHIME-WAZA*
- 1st Strangulation: KATA-JUJI-JIME (Half-cross Necklock)
- 7th Strangulation: HADAKA-JIME (Naked Necklock)
- 5th Strangulation: OKURI-ERI-JIME (Sliding Collar Necklock)
- 6th Strangulation: KATA-HA-JIME (Single Wing Necklock)
- 3rd Strangulation: GYAKU-YOKO-JUJI-JIME (Reverse Lateral Cross Necklock)

3rd Series—*Dislocations: KANSETSU-WAZA*
- 2nd Armlock: UDE-GARAMI (Entangled Armlock)
- 1st Armlock: UDE-HISHIGI-JUJI-GATAME (Cross Armlock)
- 3rd Armlock: UDE-HISHIGI (Arm Crush or Dislocation)
- 5th Armlock: UDE-HISHIGI-HIZA-GATAME (Arm Crush Knee Lock or Knee Armlock)
- Leglock: ASHI-GARAMI (Entangled Leg Dislocation)

Fig. 17

2nd KATA—PRELIMINARIES (*Fig.* 17)

TORI places himself on the right, UKE to the left of the "Joseki", as for the 1st KATA. They are face to face, side-face to the "Joseki", separated from each other at a distance of nine to twelve feet.

They salute the "Joseki" standing, and pivot a little sideways exactly as in the 1st KATA.

49

Then they face each other again to execute the kneeling salutation, or "zarei", after having advanced a step, left foot first, so as not to be more than about six feet distant.

Tori and Uke raise the right knee, the toes of their left foot bent, and assume the high kneeling posture termed in Japanese "Takakyoshi-no-kamae" (1). Their left arm falls naturally alongside the body, but it is permissible also to support their left fist on the hip at the level of the belt, on condition, of course, that both take up the same position.

The upper part of the body is straight, without stiffness, well balanced on the hips. The right hand, fingers close together, is placed with the palm flat on the right knee which must exactly overhang the right foot. The knees are therefore bent at about a right-angle. The thighs are also approximately at a right-angle and the bent toes of the left foot should then be in the rear extension of the axis of the right foot. Thus the attitude is natural and the equilibrium very stable.

Tori remains in this position. Uke lies on his back in the following manner:

He places the palm of his right hand on the ground in front of his left knee, in the axis. (A portion of this description is not quite clear and has therefore been omitted). Uke may place his left hand on the ground in opposition to the right (2) or leave it against his left thigh. He then slides his right leg between the points of support formed by his left toes and his right hand (3). He extends himself on his back, left leg bent, right leg stretched without stiffness, arms alongside his body (4 and 5). Uke is then extended on the mat in the axis of the Kata, his head near to (about three feet) and his feet away from Tori (6). Tori has not moved during all the preceding movement and the toes of his left foot have remained bent. The 2nd Kata constitutes a hard exercise and a necessary training for the knees and toes which are the points of support and equilibrium of the postures and displacements, above all of Tori.

2nd KATA—1st Series

1.—KESA-GATAME (Scarf Hold) *Fig.* 18
1st Immobilization (*Judo*, page 110)

Tori places himself against Uke's right flank in the following manner (*vide* Preliminaries, *Fig.* 6 and 7). He stands upright and takes support on his right foot in order to bring his left foot on a level with his right. He should therefore advance his left foot and not shift his right foot in order to get up; the

reason for this is that he is preparing to act and that consequently his general movement is an advance and not a retreat.

Tori shifts his position always with his feet flush with the
mat in the normal "kata" walk but no longer Tsugiashi which

Fig. 18

would have no further *raison d'être*. He takes a step to his
right, two or three steps along the axis of the Kata and pivots
a quarter turn to the left to be once again face to Uke's right
side at the height of the belt. Tori's path has followed appreciably the three sides of a rectangle but Tori has covered this
distance without any stiffness, without marking the angles,
always in a supple and continuous manner.

TORI takes up a high kneeling posture, supported on his left foot and advancing his right foot (and not the reverse).

TORI, who is then about three feet away from UKE, advances his right foot under UKE's right arm (1), then advances his left foot with his knee and toes bent against the mat.

TORI finds himself in a position of contact, right foot against UKE's right hip, left knee against his shoulder (2).

TORI, with his right hand, fingers below, seizes UKE's right wrist, lifts it, then with his left hand wedges it under his own left armpit (3).

With his right hand, palm flat, he takes support on the ground behind UKE's left shoulder close to his ear and slides his right leg forward under UKE's right arm and shoulder (4).

He ends by applying to UKE the 1st fundamental Immobilization, or KESA-GATAME (5).

UKE tries to extricate himself by taking hold of TORI's belt with his left hand and bridging twice consecutively towards his left back. TORI retains his hold on UKE's left sleeve and collar and each time baulks UKE's attempts to escape by very rapidly reversing the disposition of his legs, his left leg passing over his right to rest in front and his right leg sliding towards his rear (6).

TORI executes this movement twice very rapidly, there and back, as soon as UKE arches his back. UKE then signals his surrender by tapping TORI's right shoulder with his left hand.

TORI then releases his hold and returns to the high kneeling position (2). UKE brings only his right arm against his body in front of TORI's right leg.

2nd KATA—1st Series

2.—KATA-GATAME (Shoulder Lock) *Fig.* 19
2nd Immobilization (*Judo*, page 111)

TORI with his right hand, fingers below, lifts UKE's right wrist (*vide* preceding hold 3). He then with his left hand, thumb above, fingers joined below, pushes UKE's right elbow towards his (TORI's) right.

At the same time TORI's right knee is supported against UKE's right side at the level of the ribs, and his right foot, toes always bent, against UKE's right hip. Lastly, TORI lifts his left knee and supports his right hand on the ground at the side of UKE's left cheek (1).

UKE is therefore pushed on to his left side and TORI then places him in the 2nd fundamental Immobilizatien (2), but with his legs arranged in a somewhat different manner, the left extended forward and the right bent against UKE's right side.

UKE tries to extricate himself, at first by bridging towards his left, then by pushing his right arm towards his right, but

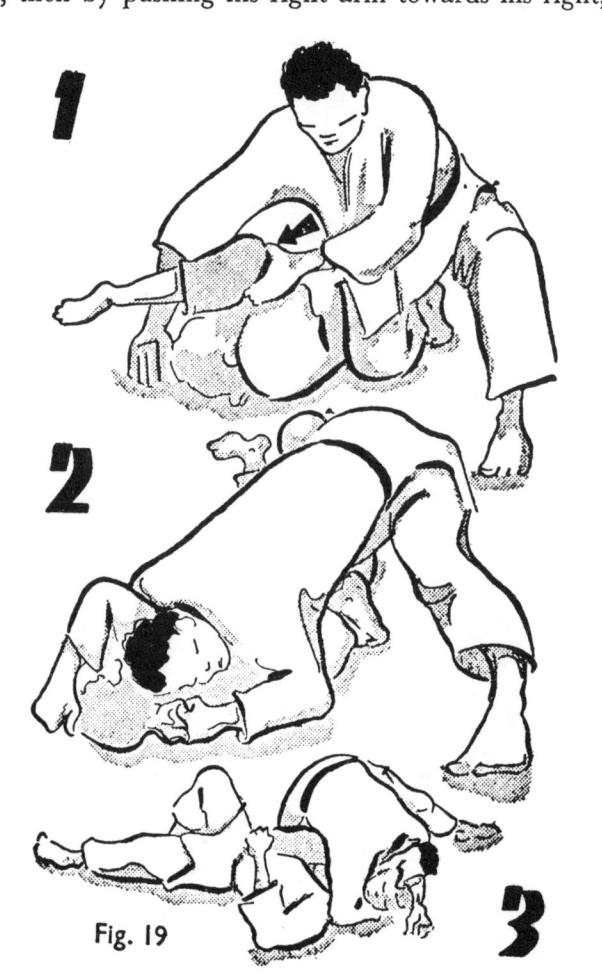

Fig. 19

without success since TORI every time tightens his hold and lowers his head more (3).

UKE gives up by twice with his left hand tapping TORI's back.

TORI relinquishes his hold, reverts to a nearby position, then withdraws his left leg, afterwards his right foot to return to the high kneeling position midway from UKE.

TORI then rises to his feet and rests on his left foot in order to bring back his right to the same level, then changes his position to return to the axis of the Kata behind UKE, i.e. he operates exactly in the opposite direction to the start of the 1st Immobilization.

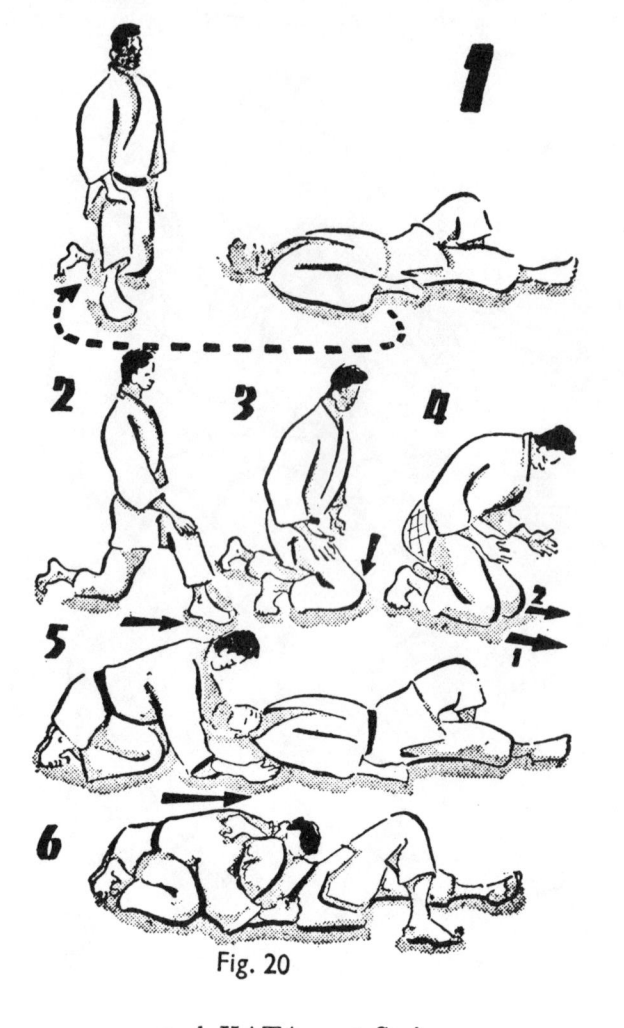

Fig. 20

2nd KATA—1st Series

3.—KAMI-SHIHO-GATAME (Locking of the Upper Four Quarters) *Fig.* 20
3rd Immobilization (*Judo*, page 112)

TORI and UKE again take up their respective positions for the beginning of the Kata (1).

Tori advances his right foot and supports himself on his left foot (2).

He lowers his right knee to the ground and takes support on his right foot which does not move (3).

He brings his left knee to the level of his right knee and bends forward to prepare his hold in the 3rd Immobilization (4).

Tori advances his right knee, then his left against Uke's shoulders and seizes him in the 3rd fundamental Immobilization (5 and 6). Tori's head is held with his right cheek against Uke's chest while symmetrically on both sides his arms block Uke's against Uke's sides, his hands gripping Uke's belt.

Uke tries to extricate himself by bridging to the left and right, but in vain. He taps Tori's back twice in token of surrender.

Tori returns to position 1 and then executes the hold in the opposite direction.

2nd KATA—1st Series

4.—YOKO-SHIHO-GATAME (Lateral Locking of the Four Quarters) *Fig.* 21
6th Immobilization (*Judo*, page 115)

Tori takes up his position against Uke's right flank, as indicated at the start of the 1st Immobilization.

He lowers his right knee to the ground without separating Uke's right arm. With his left hand, thumb underneath, he grasps Uke's belt which he raises so as to bring Uke on to his right side.

Then Tori passes his right arm between Uke's thighs to seize, thumb underneath, Uke's belt with his right hand a little below the hold with his left hand (2).

Tori's left hand then lets go its grip on Uke's belt and is passed under his neck from his right side to grip his left-side collar. At the same time Tori widely separates his knees and tightens his feet, the toes bent and heels raised (3). The position is a variant of the fundamental 6th Immobilization.

Uke has his right arm slipped under Tori's abdomen. With his left hand passed over Tori's back he grasps Tori's belt and tries with a combined effort of both arms to swing Tori above him towards his left. Uke makes this attempt twice in succession, and each time rapidly, to effect a counterpoise. Tori stretches and then closes his legs (4). Uke's attempts to escape must always be accompanied by a change of support with his feet, his right knee being raised and his left leg extended on the ground.

UKE taps TORI's back twice with his left hand in token of surrender.

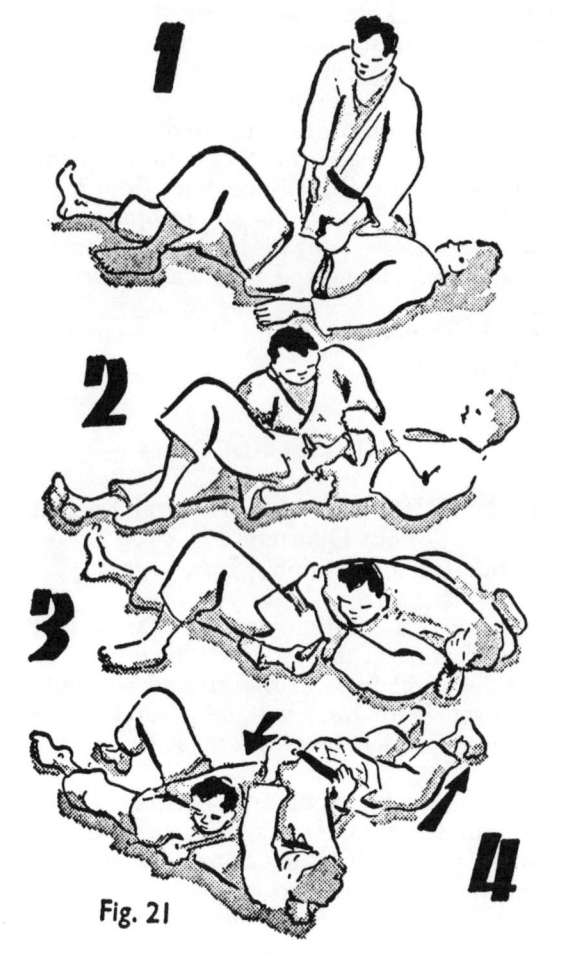

Fig. 21

2nd KATA—1st Series

5.—KUZURE-KAMI-SHIHO-GATAME (Broken Locking of the Upper Four Quarters) *Fig.* 22
4th Immobilization (*Judo*, page 113)

TORI returns behind UKE in accordance with the customary procedure and approaches him as for the 3rd Immobilization (Kami-Shiho-Gatame).

Arrived near to him, his knees against UKE's shoulders, TORI with his left hand, fingers underneath, seizes UKE's right wrist, lifts it backwards and brings it under his own armpit by passing his right arm over it (1).

Fig. 22

Then TORI immobilizes UKE in the 4th fundamental Immobilization (2 and 3). It may be added that TORI's right arm passed under UKE's right armpit grasps UKE's collar as far as possible towards the left, and UKE's right arm should be pressed as tightly as possible under TORI's own right armpit. TORI rests well forward and towards the left on UKE and his right cheek touches UKE's left flank at the level of his belt.

UKE tries to extricate himself by taking hold of TORI's belt with his left hand and essaying to push him towards his left, then to turn on his right without success. He surrenders by tapping TORI's back with his right hand.

End of the 1st Series: TORI moves off from UKE as at the end of the 3rd Immobilization (Kami-Shiho-Gatame) and UKE gets up, left knee on the ground, right knee raised, in the reverse order from the start of the Kata. As for the 1st Kata, between each series TORI and UKE adjust their judogis.

Remark: In Japan, in the execution of this Kata, UKE's attempts to escape are sometimes less pronounced. The first movement is sometimes not for the 1st Immobilization (Kesa-Gatame) but the 9th (Kuzure-Kesa-Gatame). In the 3rd Immobilization (Kami-Shiho-Gatame) the toes do not remain bent, but are on the contrary extended against the mat. In the 6th Immobilization (Yoko-Shiho-Gatame) TORI does not strongly stretch his legs as described in the author's 6th Immobilization—A, to prevent UKE from escaping, but may also block with his head in front against the ground. Lastly, in the 4th Immobilization (Kuzure-Kami-Shiho-Gatame) TORI in the first place seizes UKE's right arm with his right hand and the position of TORI's legs is less definite than as described above.

2nd KATA—2nd Series

1.—KATA-JUJI-JIME (Half-Cross Necklock) *Fig.* 23
1st Strangulation (*Judo*, page 133)

Exactly the same start as for the 1st movement of the 1st Series. UKE lies flat on his back in the axis of the Kata, his head towards TORI; then TORI places himself against his right flank in the high kneeling position.

TORI with his right hand, fingers underneath, seizes UKE's right wrist which he lifts; he then takes with his left hand the outer middle of UKE's right sleeve and places UKE's right arm on his left, alongside his left leg, in order to facilitate the contact holds which are to follow (1).

TORI then seizes with his left hand, thumb above, far behind the ear, UKE's left lapel (2).

He bestrides UKE with his right leg and places his right foot, knee raised, in the hollow of UKE's left armpit. At the same time with a big circular gesture with his right hand flush with the mat he separates UKE's left arm upwards. His hand passes above UKE's head and grips, thumb underneath, UKE's right lapel against his ear (3 and 4).

TORI then applies to UKE the 1st fundamental Strangulation (5).

Fig. 23

UKE then bends in an effort to retard the effect of this strangulation. TORI lets himself go forward, both knees on the mat and his feet hooked against the hips of UKE (6) who taps with his left hand TORI's back in token of surrender.

Remark: In Japan sometimes TORI, as soon as he is astride of UKE, places his right knee on the ground.

2nd KATA—2nd Series

2.—PRELIMINARIES *Fig.* 24

Tori has returned to place himself at the side of Uke and lets him bring his right arm alongside his body.

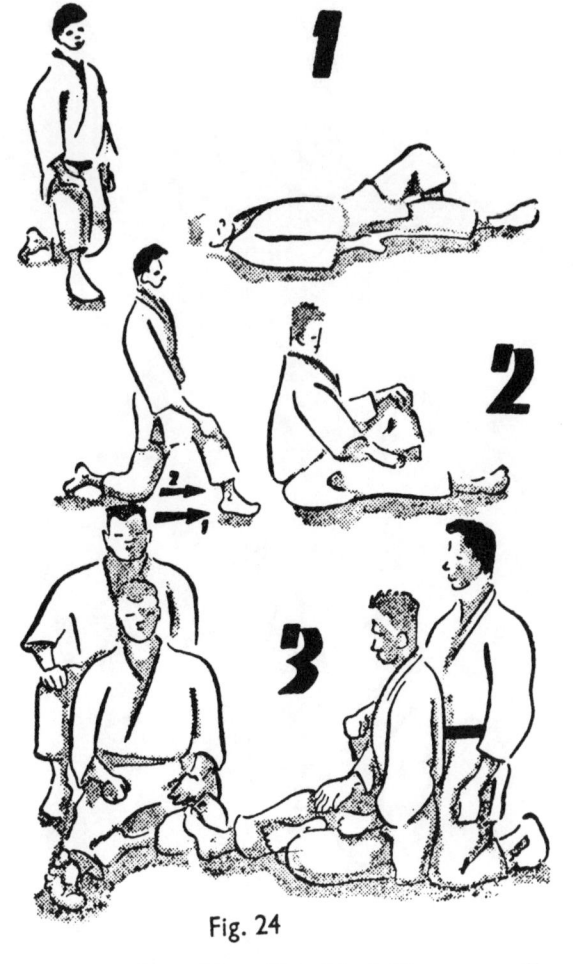

Fig. 24

He returns to place himself behind Uke according to the method already described (1).

Uke then sits up and extends his right leg and Tori approaches him to establish contact, with two successive steps, first with the right foot and then with his left knee on the mat (2).

TORI is then behind UKE against his back, as shown in *Fig.* 3, i.e. in a manner similar to the starting position of the rear strangulation (*Judo*, page 175), but TORI has his left arm extended alongside his body.

Fig. 25

2nd KATA—2nd Series

2.—HADAKA-JIME (Naked Necklock) *Fig.* 25
7th Strangulation (*Judo*, page 140)

TORI then applies to UKE the 7th Strangulation in its fundamental execution (*Judo*, page 140).

Tori can place the palm of his left hand flat on Uke's nape, as shown in (1) or else place his hand with the palm supported on his own right shoulder.

To ensure his hold Tori may also slightly withdraw his left

Fig. 26

knee so as to unbalance Uke backwards which reinforces the effect of the strangulation (2).

Uke tries to extricate himself from Tori's grip by seizing with both hands Tori's right sleeve which he pulls forward and downward; but this only slightly retards the effect of the hold when he surrenders by twice tapping Tori's arm with his right hand.

Remark: The second movement of this 2nd Series of the Katame-no-Waza is oftenest this 7th fundamental Strangulation, but sometimes it is the 4th Strangulation, or Ushiro-Jime (Rear Necklock) which is executed instead. In respect for tradition it is better to make the movement as described above.

2nd KATA—2nd Series

3.—OKURI-ERI-JIME (Sliding Collar Necklock)
Fig. 26
5th Strangulation (*Judo*, page 138)

Tori has resumed the "kata" position behind Uke. He slides his left hand under Uke's left armpit, seizes his left lapel which he separates a little forward so as to facilitate the hold with his right hand, thumb underneath, on Uke's collar behind his left ear (1).

Tori then with his left hand grasps Uke's right lapel and applies the 5th fundamental Strangulhtion (2). The strangulation results from a coiled movement backwards of Tori's right arm whilst his left arm pulls Uke's right lapel downwards, contact with his chest being maintained throughout.

Uke tries to escape, as in the preceding case, by pulling Tori's right sleeve with both hands, and then yields by twice tapping Tori's right arm with his right hand.

2nd KATA—2nd Series

4.—KATA-HA-JIME (Single Wing Necklock) *Fig.* 27
6th Strangulation (*Judo*, page 139)

Tori, as before, has resumed the "kata" position behind Uke.

As in the preceding strangulation he seizes with his left hand, which he slides under Uke's left armpit, Uke's left lapel, separates it forward from his chest and with his right hand, thumb inside, takes hold of Uke's collar behind his left ear.

At this moment Uke reacts by trying to seize Tori's head with his left arm which he lifts behind.

Tori takes advantage of this movement to apply to Uke the 6th fundamental Strangulation. Thus when Uke lifts his left arm backwards to seize Tori's head or neck, Tori advances his left forearm as far as possible behind the nape of UKE's neck, and pushes his head forward whilst he maintains the coiled position of his right arm round UKE's neck.

UKE tries to extricate himself by raising himself backwards and pulling TORI's sleeve forward with his right hand, but

Fig. 27

does not succeed, abandons the attempt and with his right hand twice taps TORI's arm in token of surrender.

Remark: Here also two positions with TORI's left hand supported against UKE's nape are possible, either fundamentally with the palm or on the contrary with the back of the fingers.

2nd KATA—2nd Series

5.—GYAKU-YOKO-JUJI-JIME (Reverse Lateral Cross Necklock) *Fig.* 28
3rd Strangulation (*Judo*, page 135)

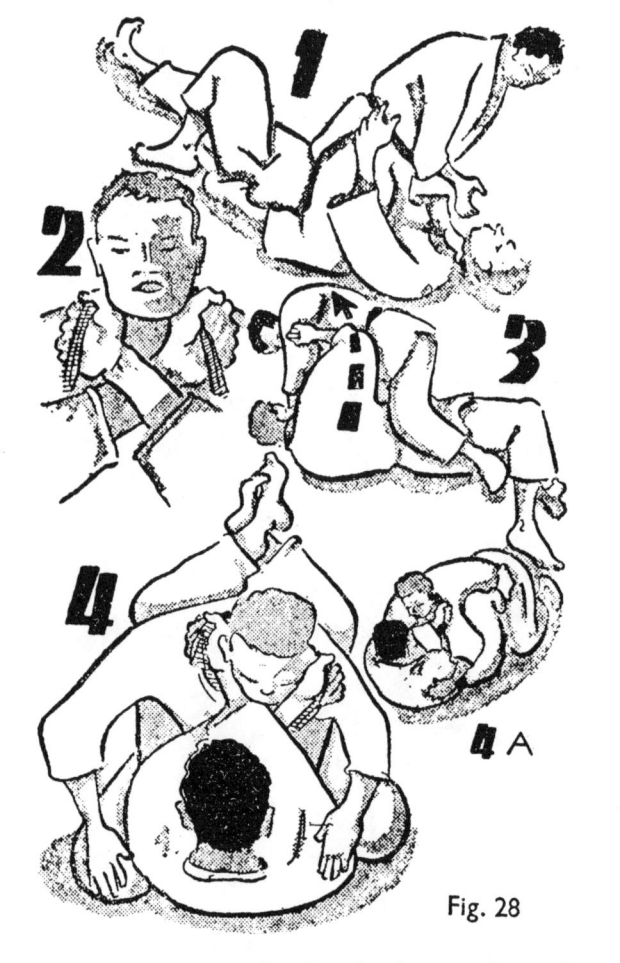

Fig. 28

Tori retreats two paces in the fundamental displacement operating in a manner exactly contrary to the start of the second movement of this Series (the Hadaka-Jime). Uke lets himself fall on to his back on the ground so that both find themselves in the fundamental position of the start of the Kata.

Tori then changes his position as already indicated to place himself on Uke's right side.

Arrived there TORI, exactly as for the first movement of
the present Series (Kata-Juji-Jime) separates UKE's right arm.
Bestrides with his right leg, knee raised, UKE's upper body.
Seizes UKE's left lapel with his left hand, thumb uppermost.

Fig. 29

Pushes backwards and upwards UKE's left arm with a wide
circular movement of his right arm flush with the mat.

And seizes UKE's collar under his right ear with his right
hand, thumb uppermost, which constitutes up to this point
the sole difference from the process of the 1st Strangulation
(Kata-Juji-Jime) executed at the start of the Series.

TORI then applies the 2nd fundamental Strangulation
(Gyaku-Jime, *Judo*, page 134). TORI places his right knee on

the ground to conclude the strangulation (1), his wrists crossed symmetrically the right above the left (2).

UKE with his palms pressing flat and strongly against TORI's elbows pushes him and makes him swing to the left beyond the axis of the Kata (3).

TORI lets himself roll on to his back and without relinquishing his hold with his hands on UKE's neck clips UKE's torso scissor fashion with his legs in the 13th Strangulation (Dojime, *Judo*, page 149).

This double hold constitutes the 3rd Strangulation (4).

Admissible Variant: Instead of the scissors to the body TORI blocks UKE's hips and flanks with his tightened feet and knees (4-A).

2nd KATA—3rd Series

1.—UDE-GARAMI (Entangled Armlock) *Fig.* 29
2nd Armlock (*Judo*, page 180)

UKE lies on his back and TORI places himself at his right side in a high kneeling position already described.

TORI does not busy himself with displacing UKE's right arm (this is, however, a variant sometimes wrongly admitted in Japan but which is superfluous).

UKE lifts his left arm as if to seize TORI's collar.

TORI then with his left hand, fingers uppermost, blocks UKE's left wrist (1) and presses it on the ground.

UKE's arm and forearm then form a right-angle; his forearm is parallel to the axis of the Kata and UKE's left hand, palm directed upwards, is blocked against the mat almost at the level of UKE's left ear.

TORI then extends his right leg and applies to UKE the 2nd Armlock of the 1st Position (Ude-Garami) in its fundamental execution (2 and 3).

UKE bends back in an effort to retard the effect of the hold but without success; he then gives up by tapping TORI's back twice with his free right hand.

2nd KATA—3rd Series

2.—UDE-HISHIGI-JUJI-GATAME (Cross Armlock)
Fig. 30
1st Armlock (*Judo*, page 179)

TORI remains in the high kneeling position; UKE replaces his left arm alongside his body.

Uke lifts his right arm as though to seize Tori's collar. Tori with his right hand pulls Uke's right sleeve, hold on the forearm upwards, and with his left hand presses downwards Uke's right lapel gripped at the level of his collar (1).

Fig. 30

Uke is thus placed on his left flank and Tori applies the 1st Armlock of the 1st Position in its fundamental execution (2). For a detailed description of this effective Armlock the reader is referred to the same author's *My Method of Judo*, or *Judo* for short, page 179. However, the attached drawings are more or less self-explanatory.

Uke bends back to retard the effect of the hold (3), then taps Tori's right knee twice with his left hand in token of surrender.

2nd KATA—3rd Series

1.—UDE-HISHIGI-UDE-GATAME (Arm Dislocation or Crush) *Fig.* 31
3rd Armlock (*Judo*, page 182)

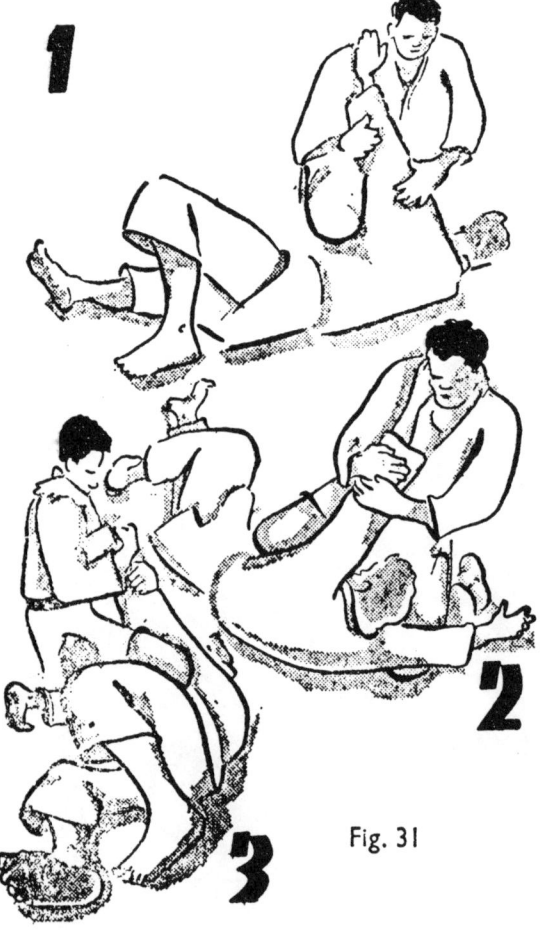

Fig. 31

Tori has returned to the high kneeling position and Uke has brought back his arms alongside his body.

Uke turns himself slightly to his right and with his left hand, the arm extended, tries to grasp Tori's right lapel (1).

Tori slides his palms "groove-wise" along Uke's arms as far as his elbow; he presses his right knee against Uke's side to maintain contact and inflicts on him the 3rd Armlock of he 1st Position, fundamental form (2 and 3).

TORI should complete the action of his hands with his wrists bent hook-wise and his elbows should remain against his body. Lastly, he should block UKE's left hand on his right collar-bone between his right cheek and shoulder and draw himself up so as to turn UKE more or less on to his right side (3).

Fig. 32

2nd KATA—3rd Series

4.—UDE-HISHIGI-HIZA-GATAME (Knee Armlock)
Fig. 32
5th Armlock (*Judo*, page 216)

TORI replaces himself behind UKE who is stretched on his back in the axis of the Kata.

Uke rises, his right knee lifted, as if the Series had ended.

Tori and Uke are then face to face in the high kneeling position at a distance of about three feet from each other. Simultaneously they advance a step with the right foot, then bring their left knees again flush with the mat.

They are midway and seize each other in the fundamental hold of Judo but in the posture of Kata on the ground (1).

Tori then twists Uke's right arm with his left arm in an anti-clockwise direction so as to pin Uke's right wrist under his left armpit (2).

Tori then falls backwards and presses the sole of his right foot into the groin or on top of the left thigh of Uke (3).

Uke is unbalanced forward and Tori then presses the sole of his left foot on Uke's right flank at the level of his belt and his left knee bent blocks the joint of Uke's right elbow (4).

Tori then inflicts upon Uke's right arm a dislocation of the type of the 5th Armlock by pressing the joint downwards with his left knee. Until the end Uke must not let go his hold on Tori's judogi; he gives in by strongly tapping the mat twice with his right instep.

Remark: Uke should remain on his knees; he should not fall flat on his stomach or roll on to his side. In the same way Tori should be on his right side and not on his back.

2nd KATA—3rd Series

5.—ASHI-GARAMI (Leg Entanglement) *Fig.* 33

Tori and Uke stand up in the natural posture and take the normal hold, as shown in the illustration.

Uke slightly advances his right foot outward (1).

Tori advances his left foot far between Uke's as though to begin the 1st Sutemi (Tomoe-Nage).

Tori seats himself as close as possible to his left heel and presses the sole of his right foot into Uke's left groin (2).

Uke advances his right foot against Tori's left flank to evade the Sutemi.

Tori then winds his left leg over the outside of Uke's right leg (3) and pushes with his right foot the left groin of Uke who falls on his left knee.

Tori then drives his left (*sic?* right) foot deeply into Uke's left groin and presses his left knee downwards without relaxing the hold with his hands on Uke's judogi.

Result: Dislocation through torsion of the right knee-joint of UKE (5) who manifests his surrender by twice tapping the mat with his left instep.

Fig. 33

Remark: As for the preceding hold TORI must not relinquish his hold on UKE's judogi and should support himself on the ground solely by his left elbow and knee. This Leglock, which does not correspond to a fundamental form of the "French method" and is not applied in competition, concludes the execution of the 2nd KATA.

TORI and UKE rise, readjust their judogi, salute each other kneeling, then standing salute the "Joseki".

In the course of the preceding study of the 2nd KATA the importance will have been realized of the various displacements effected with the right knee raised, the left knee on the ground and the left toes bent. To advance and retreat in this manner gives an excellent seating of the hips, imparts great suppleness and more strength to the ligaments and joints of the knees, and cultivates the habit of taking support on the bent toes. These characteristic displacements of the KATAME-NO-KATA are therefore extremely useful since they help to improve the technique and practice of the Katame-Waza.

As regards the selected movements, they effectively comprise the essential techniques of Judo on the ground, e.g. lateral and longitudinal Immobilizations, Strangulations applied directly from the front or from behind (with or without utilization of the collar of the judogi); then again from the front but in sympathy with UKE's reactions; Armlocks, on immobilization, on UKE's pushing which TORI follows or blocks, the 5th Armlock (Ude-Hishigi-Hiza-Gatame) which in its Kata form is a very important technique of Newaza, and lastly (as a reminder) a Leglock.

III

THIRD KATA
OR
GONOSEN-NO-KATA
(Kata of the Counters)

The GONOSEN-NO-KATA is the Kata of fundamental counters of standing Judo (Tachiwaza).

In Japan it is studied and practised only in some Schools and it is especially the Kata characteristic of one of the most celebrated Japanese universities, the Waseda University.

It has been created for about forty years by the Masters of this University and without doubt is practised more in France and Europe than in Japan itself.

Just as it is it very happily completes the RANDORI-NO-KATA. Extremely spectacular it can be demonstrated in slow motion.

It comprises 12 throws, as indicated in the table on the two following pages.

THIRD KATA
(12 *Movements*)

UKE attacks in:	*TORI counters in:*
O-SOTO-GARI (Major Outer Reaping)	O-SOTO-GARI (Major Outer Reaping)
HIZA-GURUMA (Knee Wheel)	HIZA-GURUMA (Knee Wheel)
O-UCHI-GARI (Major Inner Reaping)	DE-ASHI-BARAI (Advancing Ankle Throw)
DE-ASHI-BARAI (Advancing Ankle Throw)	DE-ASHI-BARAI (Advancing Ankle Throw)
KO-SOTO-GAKE (Minor Outer Hook)	TAI-OTOSHI (Body Drop)
KO-UCHI-GARI (Minor Inner Reaping)	SASAE-TSURI-KOMI-ASHI (Propping Drawing Ankle Throw)
KUBI-NAGE (Neck Throw)	USHIRO-GOSHI (Rear Loin Throw)
KOSHI-GURUMA (Loin Wheel)	UKI-GOSHI (Floating Loin)
HANE-GOSHI (Spring Hip Throw)	SASAE-TSURI-KOMI-ASHI (Propping Drawing Ankle Throw)
HARAI-GOSHI (Sweeping Loin Throw)	UTSURI-GOSHI (Transition Loin Throw)
UCHI-MATA (Inner Thigh)	SUKUI-NAGE (Scooping Throw)
KATA-SEOI (Shoulder Throw)	SUMI-GAESHI (Corner Throw)

3rd KATA

1.—O-SOTO-GARI as Counter to O-SOTO-GARI
Fig. 34
(*Judo*, page 27)

Fig. 34

The same preliminaries as for the 1st KATA (Nage-no-Kata) (it is, moreover, sometimes admissible for TORI and UKE to salute each other standing); TORI to the right, UKE to the left in profile in relation to the "Joseki".

When the salutation to the "Joseki" is done, TORI and UKE

advance towards each other until they are midway, i.e. in a
position to take hold of each other in the natural posture.
The displacements should be made with slow steps, the feet
slightly brushing the mat.

Fig. 35

Simultaneously Tori and Uke hold each other in the
fundamental natural posture. Tori advances his right foot a
half pace and thus places himself in the right natural posture,
or migi-shizentai.

Recollect that here in this Kata of Counters Uke is the
assailant. He advances with his left foot to the axis of Tori's
right foot and then attempts to throw him with the O-Soto-
Gari to the right (1).

Tori blocks the attack with his abdomen and bends his legs in the right self-defensive posture, or migi-jigotai; then supports himself on his left foot on which he pivots slightly and in his turn applies the O-Soto-Gari to Uke (2).

Uke is too far advanced to resist his attack and is therefore thrown (3).

3rd KATA

2.—HIZA-GURUMA as Counter to HIZA-GURUMA
Fig. 35
(Judo, page 29)

Uke rises to his feet again after having effected a kata fall. He does not return to the initial spot where he was when he made his first attack with the O-Soto-Gari, but remains where he was when he rose to his feet, i.e. approximately at the place occupied by Tori at the beginning of the preceding movement.

Tori is now to the left of the "Joseki" and Uke to the right, side face.

Tori assumes the left natural posture, or hidari-shizentai.

Uke attacks with the Hiza-Guruma to the right, i.e. with his left leg on Tori's right leg (1).

Tori withdraws his right leg a half pace to ward off the attack and unbalances Uke to his right front (2).

Then in his turn he attacks Uke with the Hiza-Guruma to the right (3) and throws him (4).

3rd KATA

3.—DE-ASHI-BARAI (Judo, page 28) as Counter to
O-UCHI-GARI (Judo, page 32)
Fig. 36

Tori places himself in the left natural posture, or hidari-shizentai, his legs somewhat separated.

Uke attacks with the O-Uchi-Gari, his right leg against Tori's left leg (1).

Tori blocks with his abdomen; he flexes his right leg and carries the weight of his body and balance backwards on his right foot.

Then Tori pivots slightly to the left to accentuate the right front disequilibrium of Uke, lifts him with the combined

effort of his forearms and wrists and with his left leg sweeps
both UKE's legs towards his own right front (2). The sole of
TORI's left foot turned upwards in the course of this movement chiefly sweeps UKE's left ankle.

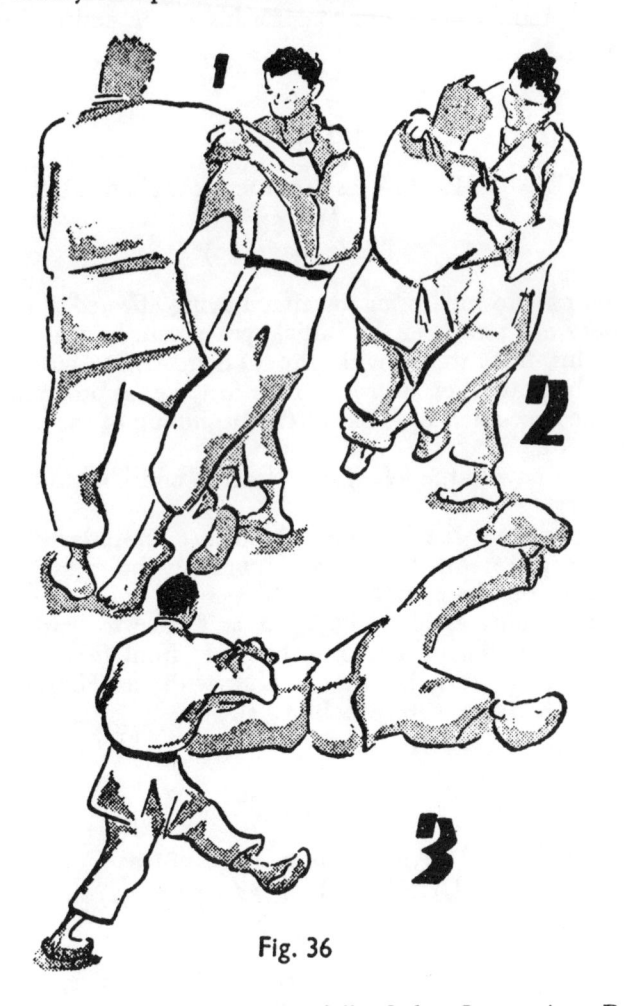

Fig. 36

UKE executes a kata lateral fall of the OKURI-ASHI-BARAI
(Sweeping Ankle Throw) (3).

Remark: This throw originates at one and the same time
from the DE-ASHI-BARAI and the OKURI-ASHI-BARAI in the
sense that it begins rather like the former and ends more like
the latter. But the sweeping action is done obliquely on both
UKE's legs, but principally on his left heel.

3rd KATA

4.—DE-ASHI-BARAI as Counter to DE-ASHI-BARAI *Fig.* 37
(*Judo*, page 28)

Fig. 37

UKE rises to his feet deliberately and at once takes hold of TORI's judogi. TORI takes a similar hold of UKE's.

TORI advances his right leg a half step to the right natural posture, or migi-shizentai.

UKE attacks with the DE-ASHI-BARAI with his left leg against TORI's right leg (1).

Tori dodges by stepping over Uke's left foot with his right foot (2) and immediately, without replacing his foot on the ground, in his turn sweeps Uke's left ankle with the sole of his right foot (3).

Uke executes a kata lateral left fall. (4).

Fig. 38

3rd KATA

5.—TAI-OTOSHI (*Judo*, page 75) as Counter to
KO-SOTO-GAKE (*Judo*, page 31)
Fig. 38

Tori is in the right natural posture, or migi-shizentai.

UKE attacks TORI with the KO-SOTO-GAKE with his left leg against TORI's right leg (1).

TORI then pivots a half turn to his left and takes support on his left foot, as shown in 2 and 3.

At the same time with his wrists he amplifies and deflects UKE's frontal movement and ends by throwing UKE with the TAI-OTOSHI to the right (4).

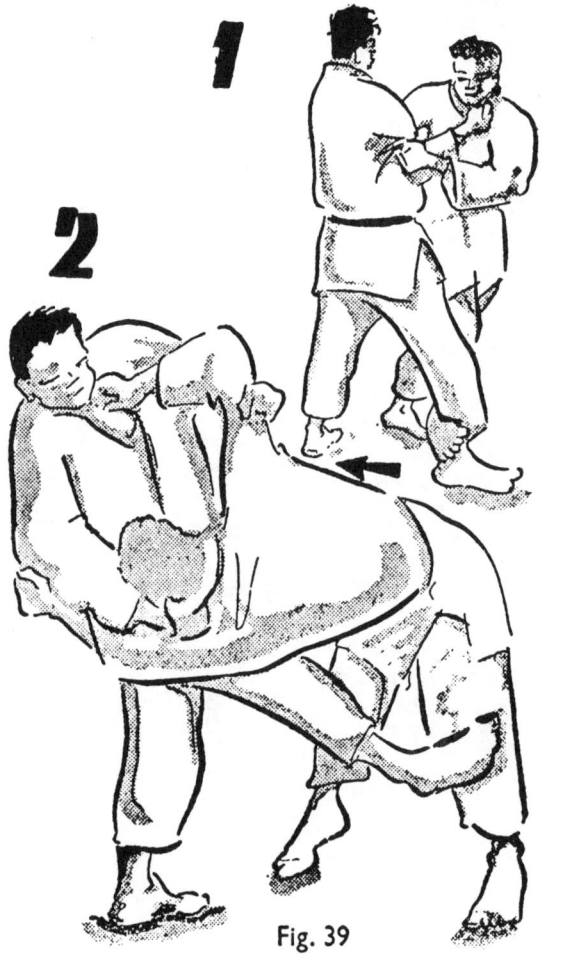

Fig. 39

3rd KATA

6.—SASAE-TSURI-KOMI-ASHI (*Judo*, page 38)
as Counter to KO-UCHI-GARI (*Judo*, page 33) *Fig.* 39

TORI in the right natural posture, or migi-shizentai.

UKE attacks him with the KO-UCHI-GARI with his right foot against TORI's right ankle (1).

TORI reposes his entire balance on his left foot and takes advantage of UKE's advance towards his left to apply the SASAE-TSURI-KOMI-ASHI to UKE's left leg (2).

Fig. 40

3rd KATA

7.—USHIRO-GOSHI (*Judo*, page 52)
as Counter to
KUBI-NAGE (*Judo*, page 46) *Fig.* 40

TORI is in the right natural posture.

UKE attacks him with the KUBI-NAGE to the right (1).

But TORI does not let himself be unbalanced forward; he resists with his abdomen, then bends his legs in the jigo-hontai, or fundamental self-defensive posture, with his balance on his heels.

Fig. 41

At the same time with his right hand he seizes UKE's belt in front of UKE's stomach (2). TORI's left hand and forearm encircle UKE from behind and rest against his waist and back.

TORI then bends still more on his legs and taking advantage of UKE's left lateral rear disequilibrium lifts him high on his protruded stomach and on his left hip with a not fundamental USHIRO-GOSHI since his head remains in front of UKE's right shoulder (3).

TORI lifts UKE as high as possible above his shoulders; UKE stretches his legs so that his fall may be more effective (4) and TORI pivoting a little to his left throws UKE in front of himself and a little to his left.

3rd KATA

8.—UKI-GOSHI (*Judo*, page 45)
as Counter to
KOSHI-GURUMA (*Judo*, page 48) *Fig.* 41

TORI places himself in the hidari-shizentai, or left natural posture, his left foot a little in front.

UKE attacks him with the KOSHI-GURUMA to the right and gets as far as the end of his entry (1 and 2).

TORI blocks with his abdomen, bending his knees and pushing UKE back with his arms (2).

TORI then repasses in front of UKE, stepping past UKE's right foot first with his right and then with his left foot. His left arm encircles UKE's waist and he makes the rotative body movement technically known as tai-sabaki from the stomach and hips (3).

UKE is at this moment unbalanced laterally left front and TORI avails himself of the opportunity to apply the UKI-GOSHI to the left (4) and throw him.

3rd KATA

9.—SASAE-TSURI-KOMI-ASHI (*Judo*, page 38)
as Counter to
HANE-GOSHI (*Judo*, page 51) *Fig.* 42

TORI is in the migi-shizentai, or right natural posture, his right foot a little forward.

UKE attacks him with the HANE-GOSHI to the right (1).

But TORI blocks and dodges with tai-sabaki to the right, very quickly advances his right foot, then his left and displaces his hips with a small turning movement towards his right front (2).

Then TORI takes support on his left foot and left bent leg

and utilizing UKE's left front disequilibrium applies the SASAE-TSURI-KOMI-ASHI to the left (3) and throws him.

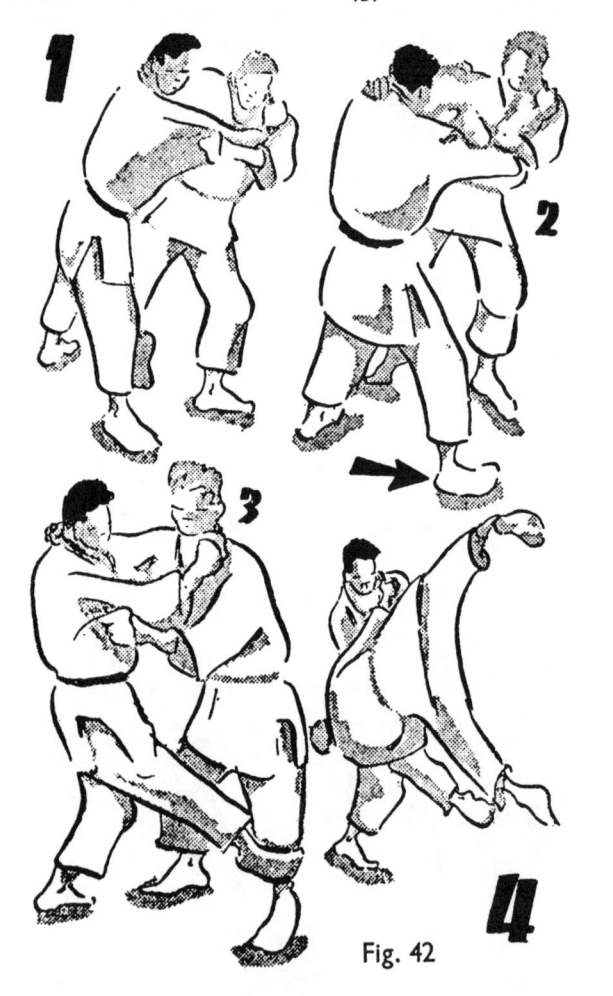

Fig. 42

3rd KATA

10.—UTSURI-GOSHI (*Judo*, page 55)
as Counter to
HARAI-GOSHI (*Judo*, page 49) *Fig.* 43

TORI is in the natural posture.

UKE attacks him with the HARAI-GOSHI to the right and is going to the end of his entry; in other words, TORI does not dodge the attack (1).

Tori blocks with his abdomen, and flexes his legs. Uke butts against him, is repulsed and so to speak "rebounds" against Tori's "hara" (stomach). Tori takes advantage of this opportunity to pull and lift Uke very strongly towards

Fig. 43

his left back (2). The pivot of the effort is Tori's stomach and left hip.

Uke is thus lifted with Tori's left hip and shoulder as high as possible backwards (3).

Tori at this precise moment advances his left foot so as to place his hips under the stomach of Uke who begins his descending movement, and Tori throws him with the Utsuri-Goshi to the left (4).

3rd KATA

11.—SUKUI-NAGE (*Judo*, page 78)
as Counter to
UCHI-MATA (*Judo*, page 56) *Fig.* 44

Fig. 44

TORI is in the natural posture with his legs somewhat
separated.

UKE applies the UCHI-MATA to the right which TORI
blocks by flexing his legs and carrying his balance principally
on his left foot (1).

When UKE straightens his back to resume the right natural

posture TORI continues to bend his legs and unbalances UKE towards his right back, i.e. towards TORI's left back.

TORI does not change the hold with his left hand on UKE's right shoulder—the only difference for the throw which is going to follow with the fundamental execution—and slides his right forearm far between UKE's legs so that his right hand can seize UKE's belt from behind or press strongly against his loins (2).

TORI finishes by swinging UKE with the SUKUI-NAGE (3) and throws him to the ground.

3rd KATA

12.—SUMI-GAESHI (*Judo*, page 93)
as Counter to
KATA-SEOI (*Judo*, page 67) *Fig.* 45

TORI is in the right natural posture, his right foot a little in front and his legs somewhat separated.

UKE attacks him with the KATA-SEOI to the right (1).

TORI very quickly makes a large rotative evading movement with a half turn forward from right to left around UKE's right hip. His right heel is at first placed on the ground far between UKE's feet and TORI lets himself fall to the ground on his back and left side (2).

TORI continues his turning movement and throws UKE with the SUMI-GAESHI (3).

UKE executes a forward kata fall (4) which he blocks on the ground (5). This fall terminates the execution of the 3rd KATA.

TORI and UKE slowly rise to their feet together, regain their respective starting places, readjust their judogi, salute each other just as they did at the start (either kneeling or standing) and then salute the "Joseki" standing.

Remark: When TORI pivots round UKE's right hip it is his right heel which must touch the mat first, since otherwise in competition the point would be counted against him.

Unlike the other Katas the 3rd KATA is not composed of several distinct Series. UKE directs at TORI successively 6 attacks in leg movements, 5 attacks in hip movements, and 1 attack with the shoulder. TORI's counters are mostly leg and hip throws.

In order to display to the best advantage the spectacular aspect of the Kata strict co-operation and a perfect understanding between TORI and UKE, the result of serious training, are necessary. But this is true for all the Katas and the 3rd Kata, even when executed in slow motion, is not the most difficult. Its chief difficulty undoubtedly resides precisely in the fact that, under the pretext of making the spectacle,

Fig. 45

TORI and UKE must not lapse into an artificial style which would deprive the attacks and counters of their truth.

Three phases should be distinguished. In each movement:

TORI assumes the posture which conforms to the attack he has to undergo;

UKE directs the attack on him truly and sincerely, but TORI expects it and that is his advantage;

TORI counters with still more determination, power and speed. It is a little reminiscent of the rhythm of the kiai of attack and defence of the KIME-NO-KATA which we are going to study next.

UKE must facilitate TORI's throws not by exaggerating and bungling his attacks, his displacements or his disequilibriums but simply by participating in the spirit of the counter by placing himself "in the way", in the direction of the movement, with his entire body. UKE should endeavour to make effective kata falls and TORI on his part must accompany him until the end of the throw.

IV

FOURTH KATA
OR
KIME-NO-KATA
(Kata of Self-Defence)

The KIME-NO-KATA, Kata of Self-Defence, is also called
SHINKEN-SHOBU-NO-KATA, or Kata of Combat.

It constitutes the synthesis of the simplest and most efficacious methods of defence against attacks with the naked hand
or side-arms, dagger and sword, in seated or standing positions.

Its proper execution demands great attention, above all on
the part of Occidentals who are less accustomed than Orientals
to the squatting posture and to whom therefore the Kime-no-
Kata seems more artificial, particularly in its first series—
IDORI.

I advise judoka to study this Kata at first in slow motion
and to apply themselves carefully to all the details, then to
train more and more rapidly, emphasizing the two beats:
attack-action and defence-reaction, and to put rhythm into
the action in consequence with the two "Kiai". The spirit of
the Kime-no-Kata, as its second name clearly shows, is that
of true combat.

To accustom himself to defence against a dagger and
sword the judoka should at first use imitation weapons, then
substitute real ones for them; the truth and quality of the Kata,
the mastership of the performers will be improved thereby.

This Kata is old; it dates from the 15th century. It constitutes the physical and moral preparation for hand-to-hand
combat, training and exaltation at one and the same time
immediately before the start of the action. It comprises 20
movements, as indicated in the table on page 95.

The understanding and execution of the 4th Kata pre-
suppose a good knowledge of all the techniques of Judo,
especially of the Strangulations and Locks, and also of Self-
Defence and the Atemis.

Also in the explanations which follow, in principle intended
for already experienced judoka, this knowledge is therefore
supposed to be acquired, and only the essential elements will
be recalled to refer the reader to the information furnished in
the earlier works of *Judo* and *Self-Defence*.

The rhythm of the KIME-NO-KATA is as follows:

Concentration before the action during several seconds by TORI and UKE preceding each movement;

Rapid and violent attack by UKE;

Parry and defence still more rapid and decisive by TORI who holds UKE mastered during several instants; then UKE signifies his surrender by lightly tapping TORI with his hand two or three times except in the movements whose conclusion is a throw or a figurative atemi.

UKE's attack and TORI's parry are accompanied with the Kiai, the second more powerful than the first. The Kiai is defined as a sort of cry more or less shrill emanating from the tanden, or lower abdomen, the point of concentration of all mental and physical energy of the individual. It corresponds more to a rapid and complete expiration than to a true cry and constitutes an auto-exaltation to bring the action undertaken rapidly, completely and definitively to an end by liberating all the available energy and immediately throwing "all one's forces into the battle" without mental reservation, once the decision has been taken. Accessorily the cry intimidates the adversary and paralyses him for a few brief moments.

Remark: Certain defence techniques are repeated several times in the two positions, seated and standing.

FOURTH KATA
(20 *Movements*)

DEFENCE SEATED—IDORI
(8 *Movements*)

1.	RYOTE-DORI	Hold with both hands
2.	TSUKKAKE	Blow with fist to the stomach
3.	SURI-AGE	Glancing blow against the face
4.	YOKO-UCHI	Blow with fist from the side
5.	USHIRO-DORI	Hold on shoulders from behind
6.	TSUKKOMI	Thrust to the stomach
7.	KIRI-KOMI	Cut with edge on the head
8.	YOKO-TSUKI	Thrust with point from the side

DEFENCE STANDING—TACHI-AI
(12 *Movements*)

1.	RYOTE-DORI	Hold with both hands
2.	SODE-TORI	Hold on the sleeve
3.	TSUKKAKE	Blow with fist to the face
4.	TSUKI-AGE	Blow with fist from below upwards (upper-cut)
5.	SURI-AGE	Glancing blow against the face
6.	YOKO-UCHI	Blow with fist from the side
7.	KE-AGE	Kick to the lower abdomen
8.	USHIRO-DORI	Hold on shoulders from behind
9.	TSUKKOMI	Thrust to the stomach
10.	KIRI-KOMI	Cut with edge on the head
11.	NUKI-KAKE	Blockage of sword in the sheath
12.	KIRI-OROSHI	To cleave with the sword

4th KATA

4th KATA—PRELIMINARIES

Fig. 46

Tori and Uke are standing and facing each other at a distance of approximately 12 feet, Tori to the right, Uke to the left, side face in relation to the "Joseki". Uke holds together in his right hand at the level of his belt the sword called katana in Japanese, and the dagger called tanto in Japanese, the guards in front and on top, the points behind and underneath (1).

They make together, while slightly pivoting, Tori to the left, Uke to the right, a standing salutation to the "Joseki", then resume their positions facing each other.

They take together the kneeling ceremonial posture, at first the left knee on the ground at the level of the right heel, then the right knee, the toes bent and extended along the mat, and finally Tori and Uke completely bend their knees, which had hitherto remained at a right-angle, and seat themselves on their heels (2).

Uke then arranges the sword and dagger to the right of his right hip, parallel to the axis of the Kata, the sword on the outside and the dagger nearer to his right leg, the guards always in front and the edges directed towards himself on the inside (3).

Tori and Uke salute each other kneeling. Uke takes the sword and dagger in his right hand, rises to his feet, makes a semi-turn to the left so as to turn his back on Tori and advances—that is to say he withdraws from Tori, six to nine feet, to reach the end of the axis of the Kata, to the left in relation to the "Joseki", towards where he, Uke, has made his way on the mat to execute the Kata.

Uke then resumes the ceremonial kneeling posture, toes extended, turning his back on Tori, therefore in left profile in relation to the "Joseki" and on the extreme left of the axis of the Kata.

Uke ceremoniously arranges the sword and dagger in front of him, perpendicularly in relation to the axis of the Kata, the guards towards the "Joseki", the edges directed towards himself, that is to say towards the interior of the mat, and the dagger on the outside in relation to the sword (4). The sword and dagger should at first touch the mat vertically by the points, then they are slowly extended on the ground. In any

case the guard must not be lower than the point in the course
of these various manipulations.

UKE rises to his feet and wends his way, in the axis of the
Kata, towards TORI. The latter has also risen to approach him

Fig. 46

and both meet in the middle of the axis, where they stop midway from each other.

They resume the ceremonial kneeling posture, toes extended;
they approach each other again, resting, arms stretched, on
their clenched fists until they are face to face with each other
with their knees not farther away than four to eight inches.
In the last displacement, knees trailing on the ground (dis-

placement called "hiza-zume"), TORI and UKE should bend
their heads to the right so as not to bang their heads together
(5). The right and left knees must be separated at a distance
of two closed fists placed side by side. This typical posture of

Fig. 47

the 4th Kata, on the knees, face to face, of TORI and UKE, is
called TAIZA.

All these preliminaries completed, which should be executed
with much dignity but without affectation, TORI and UKE
inhale deeply and concentrate a few seconds the better to
place themselves in the Kiai atmosphere of this Kata of
combat.

Remark: The reason why the sword is always placed outside in relation to the dagger is that the sword is the true weapon of combat, whereas the dagger is more a personal object, less noble in itself.

4th KATA—1st Series

1.—RYOTE-DORI (Hold with both hands) *Fig.* 47

TORI and UKE are kneeling face to face (taiza) (1).

UKE raises himself on his toes and his hands, fingers on the outside, thumbs inside, and grasps both wrists of TORI who sits opposite him (2).

TORI takes support on his left knee and the bent toes of his left foot, raises and slightly separates his arms and takes advantage of the frontal disequilibrium of UKE, who does not want to let go his wrists, to deliver him an atemi with his right foot to the solar plexus (3). The atemi is a thrust given chiefly with the great toe directed upwards.

Immediately after having dealt this atemi against UKE, TORI places on him the HARA-GATAME, or Stomach Armlock described in detail in the same author's book *Judo*, page 198, but blocking UKE's left elbow well under his right armpit (4). When executing this armlock in a swift and continuous manner TORI has pivoted towards his left on his right knee and has raised his left knee.

A variant permitted for this atemi (for beginners but not in demonstration) is a blow with the knee instead of the foot (3-A).

UKE taps the mat with his right hand in token of surrender.

Remark: This lock is applied to UKE's left arm in preference to his right because as a rule the left arm is weaker and less skilful than the right and therefore less capable of resisting and dodging.

4th KATA—1st Series

2.—TSUKKAKE (Blow with fist to the stomach)
Fig. 48

TORI and UKE resume their positions as at the start of the first movement, but this time at a distance of about a foot from each other.

UKE raises himself on his toes and hips and tries to strike
TORI with his right fist held upwards in the solar plexus (1).

TORI dodges by very rapidly pivoting a quarter turn to the
right and raising his right knee.

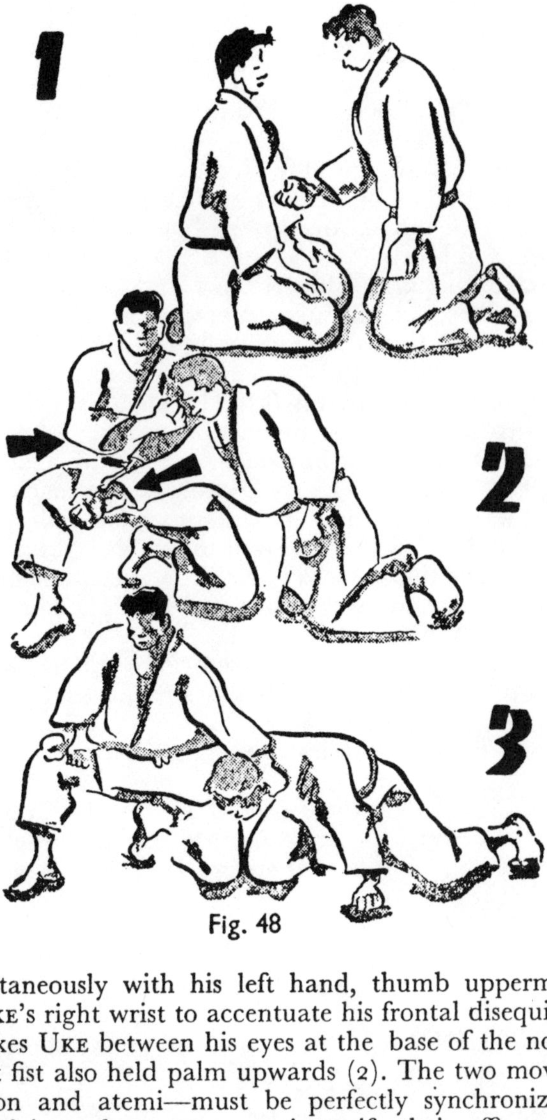

Fig. 48

Simultaneously with his left hand, thumb uppermost, he
pulls UKE's right wrist to accentuate his frontal disequilibrium
and strikes UKE between his eyes at the base of the nose with
his right fist also held palm upwards (2). The two movements
—traction and atemi—must be perfectly synchronized and
combined in such a way as to intensify their efficacy. Since
they recur several times in the course of the execution of this
4th Kata, TORI should train himself to react spontaneously,

very swiftly, in an automatic manner to the point where the evasion and atemi are executed as a reflex action.

TORI then seizes with his right hand, fingers above and thumb below, UKE's right wrist which he continues to pull forward so as to block UKE's elbow against his stomach. TORI's left hand passes behind UKE's nape to take hold under the chin the right side of UKE's collar which TORI pulls backwards and upwards, his left wrist passing behind UKE's left ear (3). There are at one and the same time dislocation of UKE's right arm against TORI's stomach (HARA-GATAME) and strangulation. This double complementary hold will be executed on several occasions during this Kata.

UKE signals surrender by tapping the mat with his left hand.

4th KATA—1st Series

3.—SURI-AGE (Glancing upward blow against the face)
Fig. 49

UKE rises on his hips and rests on his bent toes. At the same time he lifts the palm of his right hand turned in the direction of TORI, fingers joined, to push back TORI's chin and nose and dislocate his neck.

TORI also rises on his hips but bends his bust backwards to elude the attack (1).

Then immediately, on the forward impetus of UKE, TORI seizes with his right hand, fingers uppermost, thumb underneath, UKE's right wrist which he pulls forward and upwards in the direction of its push, and with his left hand, thumb and fingers side by side, UKE's right arm a little higher than the elbow. Both TORI's hands should accompany the initial movement of UKE's arm. At the same time, resting on his left knee and the bent toes of his left foot, TORI delivers an atemi with the tip of his right foot to UKE's solar plexus, exactly as for the first movement of the Kata (2).

TORI then pivots far forward and to the right, bringing back his right knee to the ground, and thus makes UKE swing flat on to his stomach, his right arm extended on the mat in the axis of his shoulder. The hold with TORI's left hand on UKE's arm has become exactly symmetrical with that of his right hand in the sense that the thumb blocks the inner surface of the triceps, the fingers remaining on the outer surface (3).

TORI presses UKE's arm against the ground; his knees and feet, toes bent, slide on the mat until his knees are on each side just behind his hands. Finally TORI slightly lifts his left knee and presses it exactly above UKE's right elbow at the level of the insertion of the ligaments of the triceps on the olecranon, otherwise the prominence of the elbow joint (4). UKE surrenders by tapping the mat with his left hand.

Fig. 49

4th KATA—1st Series

4.—YOKO-UCHI (Blow with fist from side)
Fig. 50

UKE rises on his hips, rests on his bent toes and pivots a little towards his right in order to give the blow which is to

follow the necessary impetus. With his right fist he attacks
TORI as though to plant a blow from right to left and from
above downwards, therefore obliquely, against TORI's left
temple (1).

Fig. 50

TORI dodges this attack by bending to his left. He supports
himself on his left knee and bent toes of his left foot, advances
his right foot to the side and against UKE's right knee, and
raises his right knee which presses against UKE's right hip.
At the same time, since all his movements are simultaneous,
TORI slips his head under UKE's right arm so as to block
UKE's armpit with his nape; his right arm passes in front of

UKE's head and left cheek, scarf-wise, to pin the one against the other—UKE's head and right shoulder. Lastly, TORI's left hand, palm flat, is pressed behind UKE's right hip (2).

TORI then pushes back and swings UKE with force towards his right back (TORI's left front) terminating almost in a KATA-GATAME, or Shoulder Lock (3).

TORI immediately raises his bust, blocks UKE's right elbow with his left hand, "fork-wise", and deals an atemi with the tip of his elbow to the base of UKE's breastbone (4).

Remark: Two variants are traditionally admissible in the execution of this movement, viz., the first consists, for TORI, in pivoting at the end of the atemi a complete half turn to the right to place an armlock on UKE's right arm like the GYAKU-KESA-GATAME, or Reverse Scarf Entangled Armlock (*Judo*, page 206). The second, to replace all the preceding movements with a push to the outside with the cubital (little finger) edge of TORI's left wrist against UKE's right forearm, and with a simultaneous atemi with TORI's right fist held palm upwards, or as our author prefers to express it, "in supination", between UKE's eyes.

4th KATA—1st Series

5.—USHIRO-DORI (Hold on shoulders from behind)
Fig. 51

TORI resumes the kneeling posture at his customary place at the end of the preceding movement.

UKE then places himself behind TORI in the same attitude, about a foot from TORI's toes. The knees of TORI and UKE should always be separated the width of two fists placed side by side (1). TORI and UKE are therefore in left profile on the axis of the Kata to the right in relation to the "Joseki".

UKE raises his right knee, supporting himself on his left knee and the bent toes of his left foot, advances his right foot which comes to the side of TORI's right knee. At the same time he encircles TORI's shoulders with both arms (2). UKE's left cheek presses against TORI's right ear and TORI's arms are held against his body at the level of the deltoids.

TORI raises himself on his toes, deeply advances his right leg backwards between UKE's legs in a hold and contact of the KATA-SEOI to the left (3).

Immediately TORI plunges and rolls towards his left front carrying along with him and causing UKE to swing over his left shoulder. TORI's forward somersault makes him accomplish an entire turn on himself. UKE finds himself blocked on the ground with TORI across his chest, and TORI then deals him an atemi with his left fist to the lower abdomen (4).

More detailed information about atemis with the fist can be obtained from the same author's *Method of Self-Defence*.

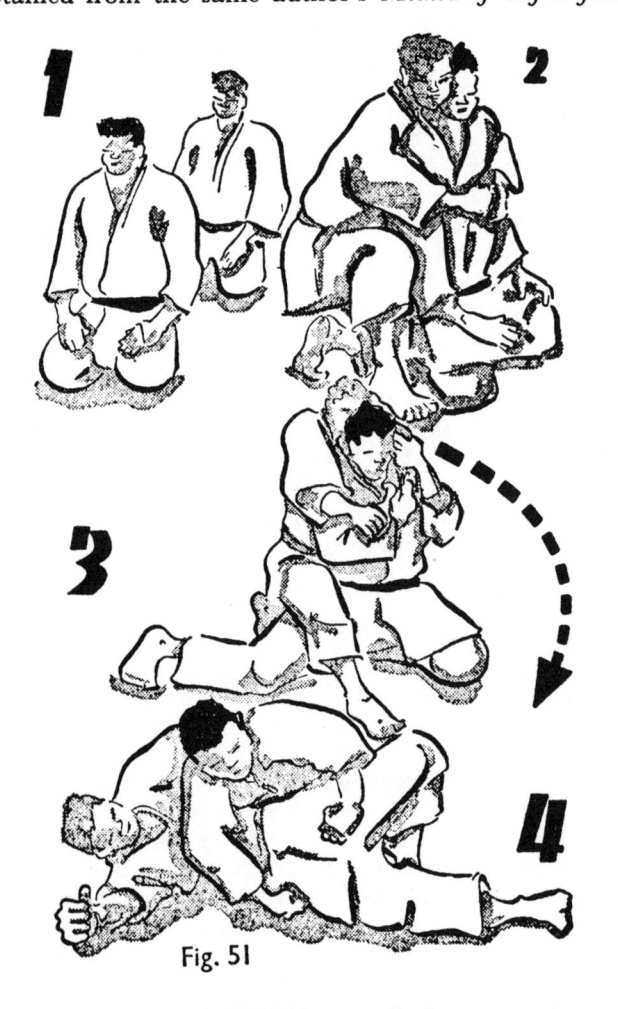

Fig. 51

4th KATA—1st Series

6.—TSUKKOMI (Thrust to the stomach) *Fig.* 52

TORI resumes his initial kneeling position. UKE goes to the opposite end of the axis of the Kata to look for his dagger. He takes the ceremonial kneeling posture, turns his back on

Tori and therefore facing the dagger and sword. He seizes the dagger and places it, the edge directed upwards, deeply inside the left flap of his judogi above his belt so that it is not visible. The fact that the dagger is placed on the left implies Uke's intention to make use of it to attack Tori.

Then Uke faces Tori on his knees at about 20 inches from him and therefore farther than for the preceding movements. Uke seizes through the fabric of his judogi the sheath of the dagger with his left hand and unsheathes it with his right hand slipped into the opening of his judogi. Uke therefore draws the dagger from left to right with the edge upwards (1).

Uke rests on his right knee and the bent toes of his right foot, raises himself on his hips, advances his left foot a pace, knee raised, and attacks Tori with a thrust to the stomach (2). All these movements are effected rapidly and in a perfectly synchronized manner.

Tori then executes exactly the same parries as for the Tsukkake, the second movement of this Series, viz., a quarter turn to the right with his right knee raised, then an atemi with his right fist between Uke's eyes, traction with his left hand on Uke's right wrist towards Tori's right (3), and lastly the Hara-Gatame armlock and strangulation (4).

Uke surrenders by tapping the ground with his left hand.

4th KATA—1st Series

7.—KIRI-KOMI (Cut with edge on the head)
Fig. 53

Tori and Uke are opposite each other midway, as before.

Uke has replaced the dagger in its sheath inside his left lapel, as at the beginning of the preceding movement. (*Remark:* Certain performers keep the sheath in their left hand against their left hip in order to unsheathe the dagger with their right hand in the most approved manner and attack as follows. Others prefer to operate as for the Tsukkomi). Uke seizes the dagger with his right hand, lifts his arm and advances his right foot a step, knee raised, and rests on his left knee and the bent toes of his left foot. Uke delivers a blow from above downwards towards the crown of Tori's head, the edge of the dagger in front, as though a sword were being used (1).

Tori, just at the moment when Uke's right arm begins its descending movement, blocks Uke's right wrist with both his hands, "fork-wise", his arms stretched upwards, as he raises himself on his toes and hips (2).

Then TORI pivots far forward a quarter turn to the right, utilizing UKE's impetus to unbalance him forward, and

Fig. 52

applies the HARA-GATAME to the right, his right knee raised, which constitutes the armlock symmetrical with that of the first movement of this Series (3).

UKE indicates his surrender by tapping the ground with his left hand.

Remark: This armlock is sometimes executed in a slightly different manner. TORI blocks UKE's right wrist with his right hand alone. He has already begun his rotative evasion to the right. TORI's left arm simultaneously encircles UKE's elbow and arm from above to block them under his left armpit. The end of the hold is the same as the above.

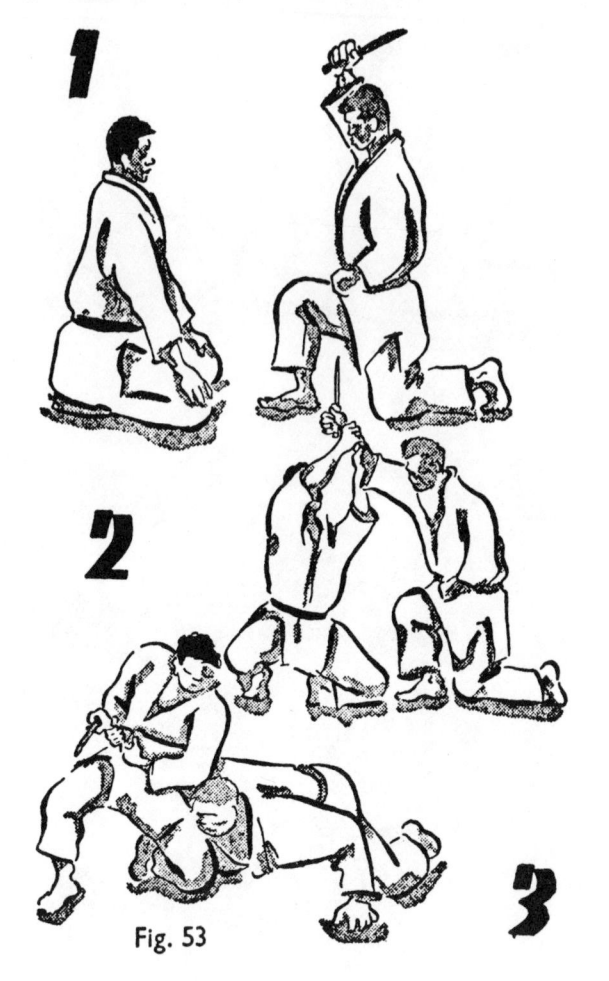

Fig. 53

4th KATA—1st Series

8.—YOKO-TSUKI (Thrust from the side) *Fig.* 54

UKE passes round from behind TORI kneeling and places himself on his knees to the right at about 16 inches and a little in front (1). Both are therefore in left profile to the "Joseki", UKE on the other side of the axis of the Kata.

UKE unsheathes his dagger exactly as for the TSUKKOMI (2) and attacks TORI with a thrust to the right side, supporting himself on his right knee and the bent toes of his right foot, advancing his left foot a step and raising his left knee (3).

Fig. 54

TORI then very rapidly pivots with a complete half turn to the right; for this purpose he takes at first support on his right knee and advances his left knee far towards his right; then, without any discontinuity of movement, he takes support on his left knee, raises his right knee which he brings back to the right back so as to place his body almost parallel to that of UKE and against the latter's right flank. The support which

Tori takes on his knees should always be accompanied with support on his bent toes.

At the same time Tori with his left hand pulls Uke's right arm forward to his right in the direction of his (Uke's) impetus, and with his left hand, thumb above, fingers below, seizes Uke's right wrist and strikes Uke between the eyes with an atemi with his right fist (4).

Tori concludes with the double complementary hold already studied, viz., the Hara-Gatame armlock and strangulation (5).

Uke surrenders by tapping the mat with his left hand.

This movement is the last of the seated series Idori.

4th KATA—2nd Series

1.—RYOTE DORI (Hold with both hands) *Fig.* 55

Tori takes up his position standing at the usual spot, while Uke replaces the dagger exactly at the place from which he had taken it, at the left end of the axis of the Kata, and arranges it in the same manner in front of the sword, the guard turned towards the "Joseki" and the edge directed towards the inside of the mat. Uke, who is kneeling, toes stretched against the ground, rises to his feet again, as previously mentioned, by first lifting his right knee, then his left, makes a half turn to the left and approaches Tori following the axis of the Kata, until he is midway from him.

Uke with both hands seizes Tori's wrists in the normal hold as in the first movement of the 1st Series (1). Tori retreats a half pace with his left foot, draws his arms from each side laterally backwards to drag Uke unbalanced forward. Then Tori deals Uke an atemi with the tip of his right foot (2) either to his lower abdomen or the solar plexus (or a blow with the knee, a variant permitted to beginners).

Lastly, Tori finishes by pivoting a quarter turn to the left and by placing on Uke's left arm the fundamental armlock (3) already studied earlier.

Uke signalizes his surrender by tapping Tori's right thigh twice with his right hand.

Remark: Like all Kata movements this should in the first place be true and correspond to reality, so that Tori, considering his position and relative distance from Uke, should be able to judge whether he ought or ought not at first to withdraw his left foot and then deliver an atemi with his foot or knee to Uke's lower abdomen or solar plexus. All this is for the purpose of emphasizing that in the execution of a

Kata that which is absolutely fundamental should be distinguished from what is relatively accessory and leaves room for a wide margin of interpretation on the part of the performers.

Fig. 55

4th KATA—2nd Series

2.—SODE-TORI (Hold on the sleeve) *Fig.* 56

Tori is standing in his usual place. Uke takes up his position midway at Tori's rear left side. Uke seizes Tori's left sleeve behind the elbow with his right hand in the normal hold and immediately propels Tori forward; both start together from the right foot (1).

Tori follows the movement, that is to say he takes two steps forward to the same rhythm as Uke (and it is precisely because he has agreed to follow the movement that he has also started from the right foot like Uke who has pushed him with his right arm).

Fig. 56

At the third step Tori, instead of continuing to advance, takes a half step with his right foot obliquely and strikes the anterior and right lower surface of Uke's right knee with an atemi with his left heel (2).

Tori immediately pivots with a complete half turn to the left (3).

He seizes Uke's judogi in the right natural posture, his right hand on UKE's left lapel and his left hand controlling UKE's right elbow and throws UKE with the O-SOTO-GARI to the right (4).

UKE rises to his feet and again faces TORI but farther away than for the first movement of this standing Series, i.e. about six feet.

Fig. 57

4th KATA—2nd Series

3.—TSUKKAKE (Blow with fist to the face) *Fig.* 57

UKE faces TORI at a distance of about six feet.

UKE takes a big step with his left foot so as to obtain his impetus forward (1).

Then he advances his right foot and tries to strike Tori between the eyes with his right fist.

Tori withdraws his right foot and pivots backwards a quarter turn to the right. At the same time with his right hand

Fig. 58

he seizes Uke's right sleeve at the level of the elbow and pulls it forward and downward in the direction of Uke's impetus and displacement (2).

Uke resists and essays to extricate himself by retreating; Tori accompanies his movement. He advances his left foot far behind Uke and applies to him the standing Ushiro-Jime, or rear necklock, and unbalances him very strongly backwards (3 and 4). TORI's right foot must be advanced from behind between UKE's legs and his left foot clearly withdrawn with a big step to keep UKE bent and unbalanced backwards.

UKE surrenders by stamping twice with his right heel.

Remark: To apply the strangulation to UKE, TORI's right arm slid on UKE's right sleeve when TORI passed behind UKE. The "locking" of TORI's hands in the fundamental hold must be completed with a blockage of the right part of TORI's head against UKE's nape. In the fundamental hand hold both hands take hold of each other with the phalanges (finger joints) bent hook-wise, the fingers close together overlapping the one against the other, each thumb in opposition respectively supported against the cubital or little-finger edge of the other hand and the first finger joint of the little finger. This style of hold is familiar to every "Catch" wrestler.

4th KATA—2nd Series

4.—TSUKI-AGE (Blow with fist from down upwards —Upper cut) *Fig.* 58

TORI and UKE face to face, approximately at a yard distance.

UKE tries to strike TORI on the chin with an upper-cut with his right fist (1).

TORI dodges by rapidly bending backwards. He seizes UKE's right wrist with both hands, his right just above his left in the normal hold. UKE's wrist is thus completely encircled. TORI stretches his arms upwards to lift UKE's fist still more (2).

Then TORI pivots a quarter turn to the right, takes a big step with his right foot towards his right to unbalance UKE forward and places on him the armlock already studied on various occasions by blocking UKE's right elbow under his left armpit (3).

UKE surrenders by tapping TORI's left thigh with his left hand.

4th KATA—2nd Series

5.—SURI-AGE (Glancing blow against the face) *Fig.* 59

TORI and UKE face each other at about a yard distance.

UKE raises his right hand with a curved movement, the palm in front, the fingers upwards to deliver with the base of the palm an atemi to TORI's nose or forehead and dislocate his nape.

TORI dodges by bending backwards (1) and even by withdrawing his right foot a little.

Fig. 59

TORI pushes away UKE's wrist with the middle of the little-finger edge of his left forearm, and with his right fist delivers an atemi to UKE's solar plexus. (*Remark:* The fist must strike held completely upwards (in supination) at the precise moment of impact, or on the contrary, according to the technique of KARATE, begin the movement upwards (in supination) so as to "twist" with a half turn upwards to the left and strike with the fist held completely downwards (in pronation). Blockage of (Uke's) wrist and atemi must be absolutely simultaneous (2).

Immediately Tori enters with an Uki-Goshi (Floating Loin) to the left (3) and throws Uke (4).

Fig. 60

4th KATA—2nd Series

6.—YOKO-UCHI (Blow with fist from the side)
Fig. 60

Tori and Uke face each other at a distance of about a yard.

Uke advances with a step of the left foot and raises his right fist. He takes his impetus to deal Tori a blow on the right temple from down upwards, obliquely. Then he advances his right foot and is going to bring his fist down on TORI's head (1).

TORI bends forward to the left and advances his left foot diagonally left so as to place himself on UKE's right flank and dodge the blow (2).

Fig. 61

At the same time he slips his right arm under UKE's right armpit and with his right hand grasps UKE's left lapel under the ear (3).

TORI passes completely behind UKE and his left hand over UKE's left shoulder symmetrically takes holds of UKE's right lapel (4). These contacts are those of the OKURI-ERI-JIME (Sliding Collar Necklock) to the left.

Then TORI withdraws his left foot with a big step to un-balance UKE backwards and completes the effect of the strangulation by blocking UKE's nape against his forehead (5). UKE surrenders by clapping twice.

4th KATA—2nd Series

7.—KE-AGE (Kick to the lower abdomen) *Fig.* 61

TORI and UKE are face to face at a distance of a little more than a yard.

UKE takes support on his left foot and thrusts out his right foot to kick TORI in the lower abdomen (1).

TORI retreats a step with his right foot and pivots a quarter turn to the right dodging in the approved manner. At the same time with his left hand he grasps UKE's right ankle (2).

TORI also seizes UKE's ankle with his right hand and draws it in front of his left hip so that he is now confronting UKE (3).

Then TORI pulls UKE's foot slightly towards his left back and therefore towards the outside of the axis of the Kata. Lastly, TORI in his turn kicks UKE, unbalanced and unprotected, with an atemi to the lower abdomen (4).

4th KATA—2nd Series

8.—USHIRO-DORI (Hold on shoulders from behind) *Fig.* 62

TORI takes up his position at a distance of about six feet from the middle of the axis of the Kata and therefore sufficiently to the right, in left profile to the "Joseki". UKE then places himself at a little less than a yard behind TORI (1).

Both advance together starting from the right foot.

At the third step UKE encircles TORI's shoulders with his arms (2).

TORI raises his arms a little and separates them so as to prevent UKE's hands from joining.

Then TORI grasps UKE's right arm (3) as for the KATA-SEOI, lowers his right hip and places his right knee on the ground, his right foot between UKE's feet and behind (4) in a variant of the SEOI-OTOSHI (Shoulder Drop).

Tori throws Uke over his right shoulder and when Uke is stretched on the ground before him Tori delivers an atemi with the edge of his right hand to the base of the nose between the eyes (5).

Fig. 62

4th KATA—2nd Series

9.—TSUKKOMI (Thrust to the stomach) *Fig.* 63

Uke looks for the dagger and acts exactly as for the corresponding movement of the 1st Series Idori, that is to say the sixth.

Then UKE returns to place himself in front of TORI approximately a yard. He draws the dagger with his right hand, and holds the sheath through the fabric of the left lapel of his judogi (1) with his left hand. The dagger should have its edge directed upwards.

Fig. 63

UKE advances with a big step of his left foot and tries to stab TORI with a thrust to the stomach. TORI dodges, as we have already seen, by withdrawing his right foot and pivoting a quarter turn to the right. At the same time with his left hand "fork-wise", thumb above and fingers below, he pushes back and pulls towards his right UKE's right wrist in the direction of his advance, and with his right fist held upwards he deals

UKE an atemi to the base of his nose between the eyes (2). All these movements must be perfectly synchronized. It is necessary once more to insist upon this essential condition.

TORI finishes the movement with the double hold studied several times already: strangulation and armlock against the abdomen, HARA-GATAME (3 and 4). TORI should advance against UKE to conclude the armlock and not to draw UKE into frontal disequilibrium as in the corresponding movement of the 1st Series IDORI.

UKE surrenders by tapping TORI's left thigh with his left hand.

Remark: The parry with TORI's left hand against UKE's right wrist is sometimes made not "fork-wise" but with the little-finger edge. It is preferable to use the traditional method described above. On the other hand, the atemi with TORI's right fist is sometimes delivered not to the base but to the end of the nose on the upper lip.

4th KATA—2nd Series

10.—KIRI-KOMI (Cut with edge on head) *Fig.* 64

TORI and UKE face each other at a distance of about a yard and a half.

UKE at once draws the dagger as in the preceding movement (or else pulls out the dagger with its sheath from the left flap of his judogi which he holds in his left hand to unsheathe it afterwards). UKE raises his right hand which holds the dagger, edge underneath and in front above his head. He advances with a big step on his right foot and prepares to strike a blow with the blade on the forehead and crown of the head of TORI (1).

TORI blocks UKE's wrist with both hands "fork-wise" at the culmination of its course just at the moment when it begins to descend and pivots on his left foot a quarter turn to the right as he withdraws his right foot (2).

TORI ends the movement with the standard armlock of self-defence by blocking UKE's right elbow under his left armpit (3).

UKE surrenders by tapping TORI's left thigh with his right hand.

Remark: Just as we have seen for the corresponding movement of the IDORI Series, the seventh, this traditional form

should be executed in preference to the variant which consists for TORI in blocking UKE's right wrist with his right
forearm only; then encircling UKE's right elbow from above
with his left arm to pin it in the hollow of his armpit. This

Fig. 64

more modern form is much less certain and is not more impressive. TORI, when he applies an armlock standing, should
at first pull UKE's arm in order to unbalance him forward,
then return against him to complete the blockage and dislocation. In the IDORI seated position UKE is at one and the
same time unbalanced and blocked against the ground,
TORI has therefore no need to return to UKE.

4th KATA—2nd Series

11.—NUKI-KAKE (Blockage of sword in the sheath)
Fig. 65

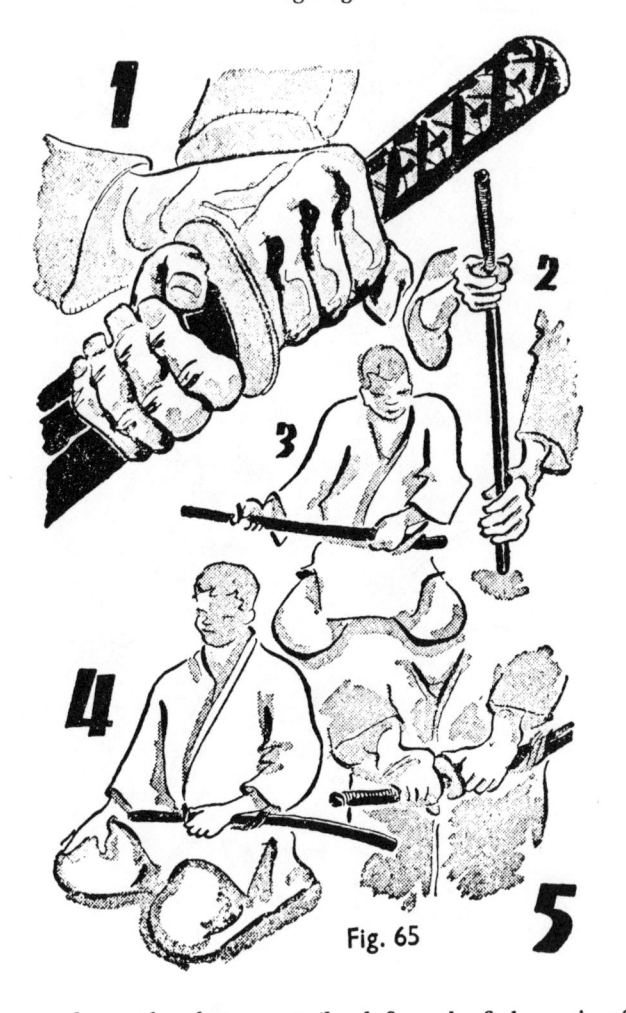

Fig. 65

UKE replaces the dagger at the left end of the axis of the Kata, the guard towards the "Joseki" and the edge directed towards the centre of the mat. Then he takes possession of the sword in accordance with the following ritual procedure:

UKE's left hand held with the palm upwards grasps the top of the sheath while his right hand, with the palm held downwards, passes above his left hand to take hold of the hilt of the sword, right against the guard. In these two complementary movements the thumbs are placed in opposition in relation to the other fingers (1).

UKE arranges the sword perpendicularly on the mat by letting the end of the sheath press against the ground; his left hand, without altering its hold, slides down to the bottom of the sheath (2) and then only lifts the sword in order to slip it in his belt from the left-hand side (3) and keeps it there in the fundamental position (4), left thumb in front.

Remark: The 4th KATA goes back to the 16th century and at that epoch the "Katana" was carried in the belt as shown in *Fig.* 4, that is to say, the edge directed upwards. If therefore the judoka should arrange it in any other manner he would be making a mistake and giving proof of ignorance.

General rule: When UKE holds his weapon—dagger or sword—on his right side it shows that he has no bellicose intention. As soon as he is going to pass to the attack he places the dagger or sword on his left which facilitates the action of unsheathing it (5).

4th KATA—2nd Series

11.—NUKI-KAKE (Blockage of sword in sheath) (2)
Fig. 66

TORI and UKE, face to face, at a distance of six feet from each other (1).

UKE takes a big step forward with his right foot and begins to unsheathe his weapon. For that purpose he holds the sheath with his left hand and the guard with his right hand in the fundamental natural manner (2).

TORI also advances towards him with a big step of his right foot and blocks UKE's right wrist with his right hand, fingers above and thumb below (2).

Then TORI passes behind UKE by advancing his left foot very far. His left hand passes over UKE's left shoulder to seize his right lapel at the level of his ear and slides under his chin.

At the same time TORI passes his right hand under UKE's right armpit in front of his shoulder and ear and presses it behind UKE's nape (3) according to the technique of the OKURI-ERI-JIME (Sliding Collar Necklock) and the KATA-HA-JIME (Single Wing Necklock) to the left. TORI retreats, always with his right foot in front in relation to his left foot, so as to unbalance UKE backwards which reinforces the efficacy of the strangulation and renders escape impossible (4).

UKE must not have drawn his sword. He surrenders by stamping on the mat with his heel.

Fig. 66

4th KATA—2nd Series

12.—KIRI-OROSHI (To cleave with the sword)
Fig. 67

TORI and UKE at a distance of about nine feet from each other.

UKE unsheathes the sword with his right hand, holding the sheath with his left hand. He may at this moment place the sheath on the ground with his left hand but not throw it. He then takes a half step forward with his right foot. He holds the

Fig. 67

tip of the guard of the sword with his left hand which is placed in the prolongation of his right hand and points the sword in the position known as "Chudan" or "Seigan" of Kendo (Japanese swordsmanship) i.e. the point of the sword is held at the level of the eyes of the adversary (1).

UKE then raises the sword above his head and advances his left foot a half step (2). His arms should at first be stretched, then he bends his elbows "spring-like" and separates them as much as possible from each side and not in front (the "Yodan" position of Kendo). UKE's thumbs should be stretched on the guard of the sword towards the point without stiffness.

UKE brings down his sword in front as though to cleave TORI, aiming at the crown of his head. TORI pivots a quarter turn to the right and executes the customary rotative evasion, and taking advantage of UKE's frontal disequilibrium seizes with his right hand, fingers above and thumb underneath, UKE's right wrist (3) which is in front of his left, in the fundamental hold of the guard of the sword, just as we have seen above.

TORI's left hand passes over UKE's left shoulder and under his chin to take hold of the right lapel of UKE's collar below his ear. During all this movement TORI should pivot widely backwards towards his right.

TORI finishes with the double strangulation-armlock HARA-GATAME already met with several times during the study of this Kata (4).

UKE surrenders by tapping TORI's left thigh with his left hand. This movement ends the execution of the 4th Kata.

UKE sheathes his sword and—if he has retained it—disengages the sheath from his belt and takes it in his right hand to indicate that this is the end of the Kata. He then regains the dagger which he takes like the sword in his right hand according to the procedure already described, and returns to place himself standing in front of TORI at a distance of about six feet. TORI and UKE ceremoniously salute each other kneeling, as at the start of the Kata, then rise to their feet, pivot slightly and salute the "Joseki".

V

THE FIFTH KATA
OR
ITSUTSU-NO-KATA
(Kata of the 5 Principles)

The ITSUTSU-NO-KATA, or Kata of the 5 Principles, is the first of the superior Katas. It represented for Professor Jigoro KANO, who created it, the "heart" even of Judo.

It is short since it comprises only five movements, which limits a little its strictly demonstrative value, and quite hermetic.

It constitutes the synthesis of all the fundamental forms of tai-sabaki. But beyond this appearance the Itsutsu-no-Kata is meant to illustrate the correspondence, the communion of these basic forms of Judo with the great cosmic principles of harmony and universal equilibrium in their continuity and their cyclic alternation.

It is in this spirit that it must be demonstrated with plenty of breadth of style and majesty, without discontinuity, without loss of time. The concentrated deliberation of preparation of the disequilibriums and their acceleration are made to succeed one another and progressively lead up to the inception and consummation of the throws.

Professor Kano did not give precise names to each of these 5 techniques comprising the Itsutsu-No-Kata either because their universality made a definite denomination in its spirit impossible or superfluous or because each form was but a partial manifestation of this absolute whole, complete, without omission or repetition which this Kata represents. However, the following names may be given to the 5 Principles in order to facilitate comprehension of them:

    I.   Principle of concentration of energy and of action (direct push);

    II.   Principle of reaction and of non-resistance (evasion);

    III.   Cyclic principle of the circle or of the whirlwind (centripetal and centrifugal forces);

    IV.   Principle of alternation of the pendulum (flux and reflux);

    V.   Principle of the Void or of inertia.

These general Principles correspond respectively to the qualities of will, suppleness, mastery, opportunity and rapidity of adaptation.

5th KATA

1.—PRINCIPLE OF CONCENTRATION OF ENERGY AND OF DIRECT ACTION
Fig. 68

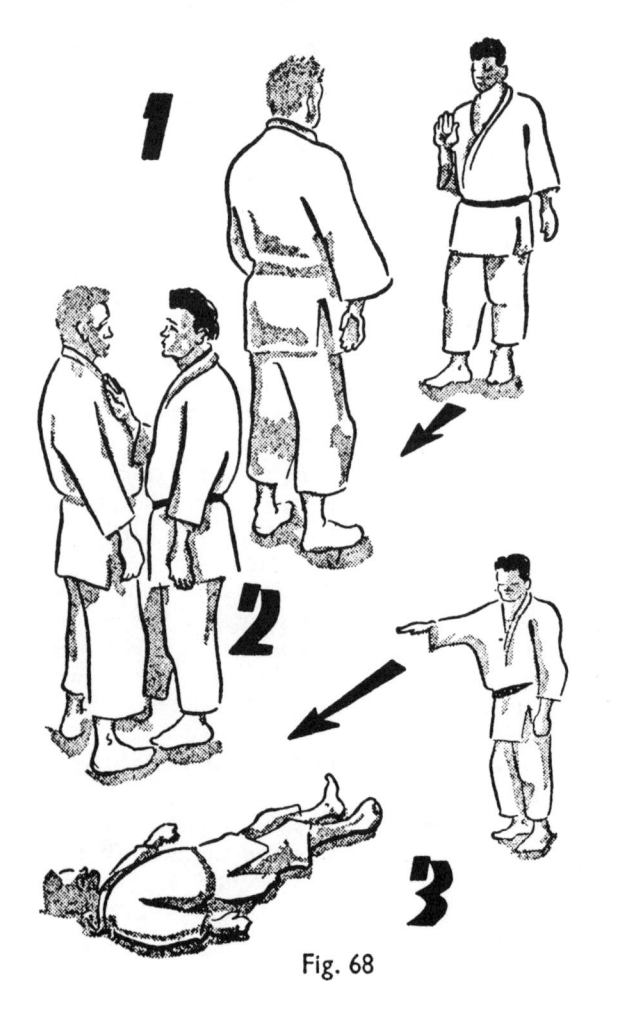

Fig. 68

TORI and UKE are standing face to face at a distance of about 12 feet from each other in profile to the "Joseki", TORI to the right, UKE to the left (in Japan it is sometimes the opposite).

They pivot simultaneously, TORI to the left, UKE to the right to salute the "Joseki" standing. Then they resume their face to face position and slowly and ceremoniously salute each other standing.

UKE does not move. TORI advances slowly towards him, his feet flush with the mat. As fast as he advances TORI raises his forearm, the palm of the hand directed towards UKE, the fingers separated at the beginning of his walk as though to concentrate in himself all the surrounding energy.

Then TORI closes his fingers which he directs upwards (1) as he continues to approach UKE.

TORI comes quite up against UKE and presses the palm of his right hand, without separating the arm from his body, on UKE's chest in the middle of the sternum (breast-bone). TORI's left flank should be a little shifted in relation to UKE's right flank (2).

TORI advances his left foot and presses the ball of his thumb against the breast-bone of UKE who withdraws his right foot. Then TORI advances his right foot and presses with his little finger and the muscles occupying the medial side of the finger (hypothenar eminence) on the breast-bone of UKE who then withdraws his left foot.

TORI continues his movement of undulatory pushing with his right hand and advances with normal and rather slow steps, but accelerates slightly and little by little stretches his right arm.

UKE withdraws with small steps more and more rapidly vainly trying to recover his equilibrium. When his disequilibrium is sufficiently marked TORI takes a last step forward with his right foot, this time quite large, and with his right arm completely stretched gives UKE a final and vigorous impetus.

UKE falls backwards like the trunk of a crashing down tree, in a single block (3) flat on his back.

TORI slowly lets his right arm fall alongside his body.

UKE immediately after his impact against the ground sits down again, bust upright, legs stretched without stiffness and separated (as for the KOSHIKI-NO-KATA which we shall see farther on).

Remark: Disequilibrium backwards pure and simple, resulting from a direct push.

5th KATA

2.—PRINCIPLE OF REACTION AND OF
NON-RESISTANCE *Fig.* 69

Fig. 69

UKE starts from the seated position which ended the preceding movement. He rises slowly to the high kneeling posture to the left, that is to say his right knee on the ground. His left hand is pressed fundamentally with the palm on his left knee. His right hand, fingers joined and stretched forward at the level of his right hip, is pointed towards TORI like a dagger (1).

Uke stands up. He advances his right foot with a big step forward towards Tori and stretches his right arm as if to strike Tori in the stomach with the tip of his fingers. Tori has not yet shifted since the preceding movement (2).

Tori pivots to the left and withdraws his left foot to dodge the blow. He seizes Uke's right wrist with his left hand, fingers uppermost, and pulls him forward with increasing impetus.

Then Tori, as for the first throw of the Nage-no-Kata, places his left knee on the ground; the palm of his right hand is pressed, fingers above, on the top of Uke's right biceps just below the deltoid (3), and Tori throws Uke with the Uki-Otoshi (Floating Drop) (4).

Uke marks a beat in the seated position the same as in the preceding movement.

Remark: Tori's right hand hold on Uke's right arm is some-times made with the fingers underneath and the thumb above. Thus Tori perhaps emphasizes a little more his upward push on Uke's arm and exaggerates his disequilibrium, but the hold itself is undoubtedly less natural than that which is described above.

5th KATA

3.—CYCLIC PRINCIPLE OF THE CIRCLE OR OF THE WHIRLWIND *Fig.* 70

Tori and Uke are in the fundamental high kneeling position at the close of the second movement (1).

They get up together, bend forward and open their arms like birds which take their flight and spread their wings!

Tori and Uke then describe, arms extended cross-wise in an anti-clockwise direction, two symmetrical complementary semi-circles (of a circle which should be above six feet in diameter) like the upper and lower loops of the figure 8 (2).

They are once again in the centre of the "whirlwind", their wrists in contact, hooked the right under the left from each side (3).

They do not interrupt their turning movement, that is to say, to be explicit, Tori, since it is he who should have the initiative and the mastery of the displacement, pivots a quarter turn towards his left followed by Uke in a symmetrical rota-tion.

Suddenly Tori lets himself fall to the ground on his back and slightly on his left flank; his legs side by side extended far forward and in contact with UKE's tibia and right instep (4).

At the same time TORI with his right wrist lifts UKE's left wrist and with his left wrist presses strongly downwards on UKE's right forearm.

Fig. 70

UKE then effects a forward Kata fall over TORI's legs and abdomen (5).

Having made a rolling fall UKE regains the standing position and TORI slowly rises to his feet.

Remark: The reader is referred for analogy to the well-known sutemi Yoko-Wakare (Lateral Separation) described on page 101 of the same author's *Judo*.

5th KATA

4.—PRINCIPLE OF ALTERNATION OF THE PENDULUM (Flux and Reflux)
Fig. 71

Fig. 71

At the close of the preceding movement UKE is at the end of the axis of the Kata and turns his back on TORI.

TORI retracts his left foot, turns his body a little towards his left back and brings both his arms parallel to the level of his left hip. He balances them supply and takes support on his hips and knees rather as though to launch a net forward, but he should not make the movement there and back but simply begin it backwards (1).

Tori slowly raises his arms cross-wise and forward like a bird which is taking flight and runs backwards with short rapid steps flush with the mat in the axis of displacement of the Kata towards Uke's left side.

Tori passes Uke a step and his arms are then raised obliquely above his shoulders and widely separated (2).

Tori brings his centre of gravity from his tiptoes to his heels, slowly lowers his left arm and his left fist presses on his hip at the level of his belt. Lastly his right arm transversely bars Uke's chest T-shaped (3).

At the same time without any pause Tori begins to retreat (do not forget that this is the movement of the wave which is never really motionless for long) and carries Uke along in his retreat, his "reflux".

Uke is progressively unbalanced backwards as in the first movement of this Kata, falls flat on his back to the right back of Tori who has placed his left knee on the ground (4), then seats himself bust upright, legs separated, while Tori lets his right arm fall slowly alongside his body.

5th KATA

5.—PRINCIPLE OF THE VOID OR OF INERTIA
Fig. 72

Tori rises to his feet again and takes support on his right foot. Uke also stands up but turns his back on Tori.

Tori and Uke both advance their right foot and widely spread their arms like a bird which spreads its wings in flight (1).

Then they begin to turn a little as for the beginning of the third throw of this Kata but with a swifter movement more direct and less circular which they end by running towards each other with short small steps skimming the mat (2 and 3).

At the moment when both their bodies are about to collide Tori very rapidly lets himself fall to the ground on his back, his legs brought together athwart the axis of Uke's displacement (3 and 4).

Before this barrier Uke is obliged to effect a Kata fall very high over Tori's body (4 and 5).

Uke comes to his feet with the impetus of his rolling fall and Tori then rises slowly in a continuous manner.

This throw concludes the ITSUTSU-NO-KATA. TORI and UKE return to their initial places, readjust their judogi, salute each other standing and then salute the "Joseki" standing.

Fig. 72

Remark: Here again is illustrated the principle of the Yoko-Wakare (Lateral Separation) which recurs on several occasions in the study of the KOSHIKI-NO-KATA.

VI

SIXTH KATA
OR
JU-NO-KATA
(Form of Suppleness)

Translator's Note: The Japanese character "jū" is more literally rendered "gentleness" or "softness" in English. It is identical with the syllable "jū" in jujutsu and judo.

The JU-NO-KATA, or Kata of Suppleness, is composed of techniques selected for training in attack, defence and the efficacious employment of displacements and energy. It is at the same time an excellent physical exercise and a complete instruction in the basic movements for beginners.

This Kata is executed in slow motion, in a continuous, supple and linked manner.

It affords the special advantage of being able to be studied in a restricted space and even in clothing other than the judogi.

Although considered as a superior Kata it is not reserved for experts or champions. Even performers less strong, women and children, can repeat it as a true preparatory and condensed physical culture of randori.

In Japan it is often women who demonstrate it. But Professor Kano insisted upon the necessity for frequent practice of this Kata.

The JU-NO-KATA is composed of 3 Series of 5 Movements each, as indicated on the following page.

SIXTH KATA
(15 *Movements*)

1st Series

1. TSUKI-DASHI (To transpierce with the hand)
2. KATA-OSHI (To push the shoulders)
3. RYOTE-DORI (Hold with both hands)
4. KATA-MAWASHI (Rotation of the shoulders)
5. AGO-OSHI (To push back the chin)

2nd Series—

1. KIRI-OROSHI (To split the head with a weapon)
2. RYO-KATA-OSHI (To press on both shoulders)
3. NANAME-UCHI (To split obliquely)
4. KATATE-DORI (Hold with one hand)
5. KATATE-AGE (To raise the hand to strike)

3rd Series—

1. OBI-TORI (Hold of the belt)
2. MUNE-OSHI (To push back the chest)
3. TSUKI-AGE (Blow with fist from down upwards— upper-cut)
4. UCHI-OROSHI (Blow with fist from up downwards)
5. RYOGAN-TSUKI (To strike the eyes)

1.—TSUKI-DASHI (To transpierce with the hand)
Figs. 73 and 74

Fig. 73

TORI and UKE are standing face to face at a distance of about ten feet from each other (1). TORI is to the right and UKE to the left of the "Joseki". They pivot slightly towards the "Joseki" to salute together standing, then they face each other again to salute each other also standing.

Uke advances towards Tori with the tsugiashi, or following foot, the right foot in front followed by the left foot and in this manner takes three steps until he is at arm's length from Tori. In the execution of this Kata in Japan Tori and Uke

Fig. 74

may at first advance together with a short step, and it is sometimes admissible for Uke's walk to be normal with slow alternate steps, the sole of the foot flush with the ground and not in the tsugiashi style. Progressively as he advances Uke slowly raises his right arm, the fingers pointed forward up to the level of Tori's eyes (2 and 3).

Tori then pivots a quarter turn to the right and with his

right hand, fingers above and thumb below, seizes UKE's right wrist (4).

TORI continues to pull UKE forward. UKE takes a step more with his right and then his left foot in tsugiashi which brings him in front of TORI. The right arms of TORI and UKE are stretched obliquely upwards (5).

TORI then takes UKE's left wrist with his left hand in the reverse hold, viz., his thumb above and fingers below (6) and bends backwards while holding UKE's arms in line (as for 11 previous page, but his right arm upwards and his left downwards).

The bodies of TORI and UKE are stretched, knees unbent, legs a little separated. UKE then slightly bends his knees, seizes TORI's wrists from either side in symmetrical holds opposite to those of TORI (7) and pivots a complete half turn towards his left (8, 9 and 10) which brings him behind TORI. TORI has exactly followed the movement of rotation by pivoting a half turn towards his right.

TORI is therefore in front of UKE. Their left arms are raised and their left arms lowered diagonally (11).

TORI and UKE then again pivot together a half turn, TORI to the right and UKE to the left, viz., always in the same direction of rotation (that of the hands of the clock for TORI and the reverse for UKE) which again brings TORI behind UKE after a complete turn on both sides (12) since the beginning of the movement.

TORI then places his left hand on the top of UKE's left shoulder and stretches UKE's right arm upwards (13).

Lastly, TORI falls back a step—right foot, then left foot on the same plane—and in this manner unbalances UKE clearly backwards (14).

UKE surrenders by striking his thigh with his left hand and TORI brings him back to the normal balanced position by advancing a step. TORI should accompany UKE's right arm which falls back gently alongside his body.

6th KATA—1st Series

2.—KATA-OSHI (To push the shoulders) *Fig.* 75

TORI is behind UKE at the close of the preceding movement. He passes round him from his left and Uke is now placed a step behind TORI in relation to the "Joseki" (position 1 viewed from in front of the "Joseki".)

UKE with his right hand pushes TORI's right shoulder (2)

forward. UKE's hand presses on the summit of TORI's right shoulder-blade.

TORI bends forward (3), then steps back to the right of UKE (4).

Fig. 75

UKE's right hand slides in front of the shoulder of TORI who seizes it in passage with his own right hand and places his thumb in the middle of the palm and his fingers covering the back of UKE's hand.

TORI continues to fall back and slowly raises UKE's hand as though to dislocate his right shoulder by back torsion. UKE evades this hold by pivoting a half turn to the right which brings him face to face with TORI and tries to deal him an

atemi to the eyes with the finger-tips of his left hand, viz.,
"ryogan-tsuki" (5).

TORI parries UKE's attack by seizing his left hand with his
own left hand in a hold symmetrical with that of his right

Fig. 76

hand, viz., his thumb on the palm and his fingers on the
back of the hand (6).

Lastly, TORI raises UKE's hands above his head in back
torsion so as to stretch his arms and recedes one more step in
order to unbalance him backwards (7).

UKE surrenders by striking the mat with his left heel, since
his right foot constitutes the first point of balance, and TORI
brings him back to the right natural posture.

6th KATA—1st Series

3.—RYOTE-DORI (Hold of both hands)
Fig. 76

TORI, and UKE in front of him, are in left profile to the "Joseki". UKE followed by TORI comes with slow steps to place himself again in the middle of the axis of the Kata, then turns round to face TORI.

UKE then grips TORI's wrists with the normal hold, thumbs inside (1), as for the first movement of the 4th KATA.

TORI pivots a half turn to the left; he advances his right foot towards his left, disengages his right wrist and pulls, while lifting it towards his left shoulder, UKE's right wrist which he seizes with his left hand fork-wise. TORI's right arm passes with a circular gesture above UKE's right arm (2) which it blocks under his armpit.

TORI, once this contact is well secured, bends forward as though to throw UKE with the sutemi MAKIKOMI, or Inner Winding. But TORI must not lose his balance or throw UKE. UKE takes support with the palm of his left hand on TORI's left hip so as to place his body extended in a right line and curves in the small of his back (3). The fingers of UKE's left hand, to facilitate the support, should be pointed downwards. TORI's knees should not be bent and UKE's legs should be joined, tiptoes stretched as for a gymnastic movement.

TORI and UKE mark a pause of two or three seconds in this position and then TORI gently replaces UKE.

6th KATA—1st Series

4.—KATA-MAWASHI (Rotation of the shoulders)
Fig. 77

TORI in front of UKE, both in right profile to the "Joseki" in the final position of the preceding movement (1).

UKE places his hands on TORI's shoulders in the following manner: his left hand is placed on the top of TORI's left shoulder and the palm of his right hand presses against TORI's right shoulder-blade (2).

UKE then tries to make TORI pivot with a half turn to the left by pulling him with his left hand and pushing him with his right hand. TORI follows the movement; he pivots on his left foot with a half turn to the left, raises his left arm so as to place his left hand on UKE's right shoulder when he comes in front of him (3).

TORI continues his turning movement until he effects a complete turn. His right arm has slid under UKE's right

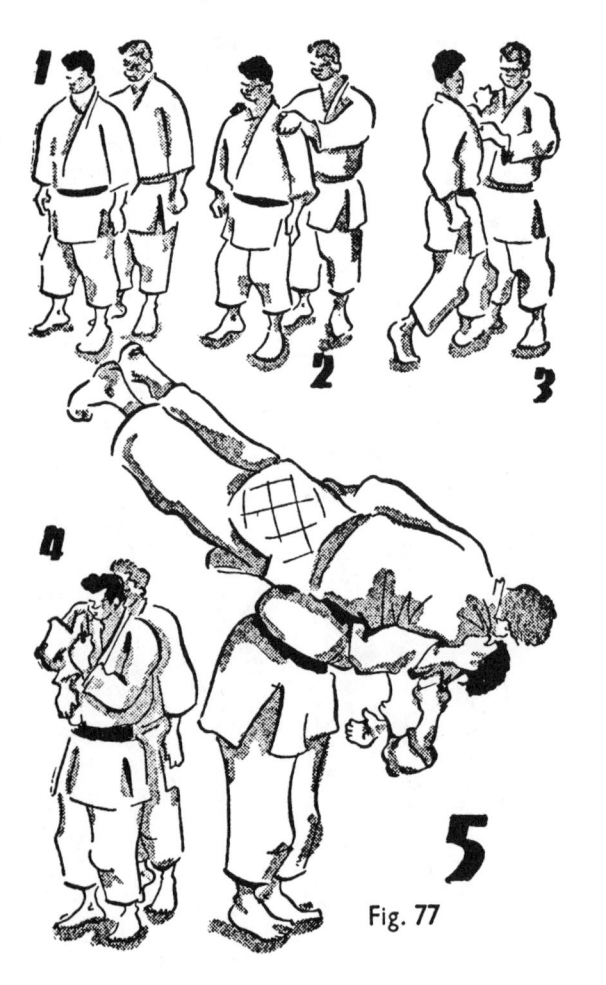

Fig. 77

armpit so that he is in front of UKE (4) in the position for the SEOINAGE, or Shoulder Throw.

TORI bends slowly forward as though to throw UKE in slow motion. UKE takes support with the palm of his left hand on TORI's left hip, stretches his body, and curves in the small of his back in a manner similar to the preceding movement (5).

Pause of two or three seconds, and then TORI lets UKE gently descend again to the ground.

6th KATA—1st Series

5.—AGO-OSHI (To push back the chin) *Fig.* 78

Fig. 78

At the close of the preceding movement TORI and UKE are in the axis of the Kata and in right profile to the "Joseki", TORI in front of UKE. UKE does not move. TORI advances two steps towards the right end of the axis of the Kata, then pivots with a quarter turn to the right so as to face the "Joseki".

UKE advances towards TORI with the tsugiashi, or "following foot" style, raises his right arm with the hand held blade-wise, palm to the left and back of the hand towards the

"Joseki", to take hold of Tori's chin and make his head pivot to the left (1).

At the moment when Uke's hand is reaching his chin Tori seizes it with his right hand, thumb in the middle of the palm and fingers against the back of Uke's hand, and pivots a three-quarter turn to his left and pulls upwards Uke's right arm (2 and 3) under which he passes his head.

Tori is again in left profile to the "Joseki". Uke tries, as for the second movement of this Series, to deliver a thrust with the fingers of his left hand at Tori's eyes (3).

Tori then with his left hand seizes Uke's left hand, always with the thumb in the hollow of the palm and the fingers on the back of (Uke's) hand (4).

Lastly, Tori lifts Uke's hands above his head and then unbalances Uke backwards by receding a step (5).

Uke surrenders by hitting the ground with his heel, preferably the left. Tori brings Uke back to the natural posture and this movement ends the 1st Series.

6th KATA—2nd Series

1.—KIRI-OROSHI (To cleave the head with a weapon)
Figs. 79 and 80

Tori, and Uke in front of him, in left profile to the "Joseki" at the end of the preceding movement, advance together starting on the left foot, as far as the middle of the axis of the Kata. Then Uke turns and faces Tori to begin the 2nd Series (1, position seen in front of the "Joseki").

Uke pivots a quarter turn to the right and is therefore facing the "Joseki" (2). Then Uke raises his right hand on this side blade-wise with the palm directed towards the "Joseki" (3). Uke has his legs somewhat separated.

Uke then pivots again a quarter turn towards the left to face Tori again and advances his right foot as he tries to strike Tori on the crown of his head with the edge of his right hand representing a sword (4).

Tori dodges by first retracting his left foot, then his right (5). Uke's right arm continues its downward movement and Tori blocks it in its course by seizing the wrist in the normal hold with his right hand (6).

Tori advances a step in tsugiashi and pushes Uke's wrist downwards but Uke then pushes Tori's elbow towards his right with his left hand, thumb above and fingers below (7).

Uke's left hand can cover Tori's right elbow or seize the fabric of the judogi.

Tori then pivots a complete turn towards the left and passes beyond Uke's pushing (8, 9 and 10) and is again

Fig. 79

behind Uke. The displacement is sufficiently shown by the drawings so that further description is unnecessary.

Tori then seizes Uke's left hand with his left hand, using the special hand-hold of the 6th Kata already several times described (11) and places his right hand on Uke's left shoulder (12).

Tori lifts Uke's left hand above and behind his shoulder

and retreats a step in order to unbalance UKE clearly backwards (13).

UKE surrenders by striking the mat with his left heel and TORI brings him back to the natural posture.

Fig. 80

Remark: TORI's left hand should seize UKE's exactly as shown in Figures 11 and 12, viz., by the little-finger edge in front and towards the inside. Afterwards TORI's hand turns around the wrist and finishes the hold against the thumb-edge of UKE's hand (13), holding the muscles of the thumb occupying the lateral side, or in anatomical parlance, the thenar eminence. In Japan it is admissible for TORI to seize UKE's wrist direct and not the hand.

6th KATA—2nd Series

2.—RYO-KATA-OSHI (To press on both shoulders)
Fig. 81

Fig. 81

Tori places himself in the middle of the axis of the Kata in right profile to the "Joseki" and Uke behind him halfway.

Uke raises his arms bent (1) and stretches them above his head (2), the palms in front.

Then he lowers his arms; the palms press on Tori's shoulders to compel him to flex his knees (3).

TORI follows the movement. He squats on his heels but while pivoting a complete turn on the left (4, 5 and 6).

When at the end of a half turn TORI faces UKE he seizes UKE's right wrist with both his hands, the thumbs pressed on the thumb edge (5), then while continuing his rotation TORI changes the hold with his left hand the thumb of which is placed on the little-finger edge (of UKE's hand) (6).

TORI then draws himself up again as he pulls UKE's right arm upwards in front (7). TORI passes in front of the right hip of UKE who tries to re-establish his balance by pressing the palm of his left hand against TORI's left hip with the fingers directed downwards.

UKE lifts his left hand from the left hip of TORI who places his left foot behind UKE's feet and whose left arm makes a diagonal barrier in front of UKE's chest (8).

TORI breaks UKE's balance by pushing him backwards and UKE strikes his thigh with his left hand in token of surrender.

6th KATA—2nd Series

3.—NANAME-UCHI (To cleave obliquely) *Fig.* 82

TORI and UKE place themselves again in the middle of the axis of the Kata, TORI to the right and UKE to the left of the "Joseki".

UKE slowly raises his right arm; his hand, blade-wise, reaches the level of UKE's left ear, the palm directed downwards (1).

UKE essays to strike TORI's right cheek-bone with the back hand. TORI dodges by bending backwards and UKE's hand passes in front of his face. When it has passed, TORI seizes UKE's right wrist with his left hand, fingers above (2) and advancing his right foot in the tsugiashi counter-attacks with a thrust of the fingers of his right hand, palm directed towards the ground, at UKE's eyes (3).

UKE dodges by pivoting a quarter turn to the right and with his left hand, fingers above, seizes TORI's right wrist which he pulls forward (4).

TORI then releases UKE's right wrist and with his left hand, thumb above, takes hold of UKE's left wrist (5). UKE then with his right hand pushes TORI's left arm or elbow.

TORI pivots an entire half turn towards his right and is in front of and under UKE's left armpit (6).

TORI clearly flexes his knees and encircles UKE's waist with his arms (7). The palm of his left hand presses against UKE's left hip.

(*Translator's Note:* Fig. 7 does not show the position of TORI's left hand. On the other hand, it does show TORI's *right hand* pressed against UKE's *right* hip.)

Fig. 82

Then TORI stands erect again and blocks UKE on his right pectoral as for the USHIRO-GOSHI (Rear Loin) and UKE stretches his body, arms and legs slightly separated (8).

Then UKE joins his legs and finally claps his hands in token of surrender (9). TORI gently replaces UKE on the ground. He ought not, moreover, to have to make an excessive effort to lift him.

6th KATA—2nd Series

4.—KATATE-DORI (Hold with one hand)
Fig. 83

Fig. 83

TORI and UKE, side by side on the axis of the Kata with their backs to the "Joseki", TORI to the left, UKE to the right (1, seen in front of the Joseki").

UKE with his left hand, with the normal hold, fingers above, seizes TORI's right wrist (2).

TORI disengages his wrist by pivoting a quarter turn to the left (3) and advancing his right foot.

UKE follows the movement in order to try to retain his hold and his right hand thus slides along TORI's right forearm and arm as far as above the elbow. UKE then pushes TORI's right shoulder with his right hand to make him pivot more towards his left (4).

TORI takes advantage of this movement to enter for the UKI-GOSHI (Floating Loin) to the left (5).

UKE is balanced extended across TORI's left hip and retains his balance by pressing his right hand on TORI's right hip or shoulder (6).

After a pause of two or three seconds in this attitude TORI gently lets UKE return to the ground.

Remark: UKE in principle indicates his surrender by tapping in the usual manner when he is unbalanced, but with his feet left in contact with the ground. When TORI keeps UKE above the ground in an interrupted and a conventionalized throw, it suffices for both performers to mark a pause of a few seconds.

6th KATA—2nd Series

5.—KATATE-AGE (To raise the hand to strike)
Fig. 84

TORI and UKE on the axis of the Kata at several paces from each other, TORI to the left and UKE to the right of the "Joseki", i.e. in the opposite position to the initial one of the Kata (1).

TORI and UKE simultaneously raise their right arms and describe an arc sideways with the palms in front, one towards the other, and place themselves on tiptoe (2).

Then always on their toes they run towards each other with short and rapid steps and meet each other, right flank against right flank in the centre of the mat where their arms cross as shown in Fig. 3.

TORI dodges the shock and clinch by pivoting a quarter turn to the right, but UKE, carried along by his impetus, advances his right foot and bends towards his right (4). TORI and UKE in front of him are then facing the "Joseki".

UKE reacts and stands erect again. TORI had placed his left hand on UKE's left shoulder (4); he makes it descend along UKE's left arm to the level of his elbow and with his right hand lifts and pushes UKE's right elbow towards his (UKE's) left in order to exaggerate his reaction and thus compel him to lean to the left (5).

UKE stands erect again (6); at this moment TORI's right hand ascends along UKE's right arm to grasp his wrist and

Fig. 84

his left hand ascends from UKE's left elbow as far as his shoulder (7).

Then TORI recedes a step and keeps UKE in clear disequilibrium backwards (8).

UKE surrenders by tapping his thigh with his left hand and TORI brings UKE back to the natural posture which terminates the 2nd Series.

6th KATA—3rd Series

1.—OBI-TORI (Hold on the belt) *Figs.* 85 *and* 86

Fig. 85

Tori and Uke are on the axis of the Kata in the middle at two paces, Tori to the right and Uke to the left of the "Joseki".

Uke takes a step with his left foot and raises his hands with an enveloping gesture, crossing the left over the right to grasp Tori's belt (1).

Tori seizes Uke's left wrist with his right hand, thumb on

top, and pulls it forward and to his left to dodge the hold, and pivots slightly towards his left (2).

TORI's left hand covers UKE's left elbow, thumb on top, and fingers directed to the left. TORI advances his left foot and

Fig. 86

makes UKE pivot a half turn to the right (3) as far as to bring him back with his back turned to TORI (4).

TORI continues to make UKE pivot towards his right by pulling UKE's right arm with his right hand (5).

UKE, after having thus made a complete turn to the right, is again facing TORI who pushes back his right shoulder with his right hand, but UKE then seizes TORI's right sleeve with his right hand at the level of the elbow (6).

UKE pulls TORI's right elbow towards his right with his right hand, and his left hand, pressed on TORI's left shoulder, completes the "twisting" of TORI towards the left; but TORI follows the movement and effects a half turn towards his left (7) to find himself again with his back turned to UKE's right side (8). During this movement TORI's right arm is "wound" spirally in front and diagonally upwards (9).

TORI then slides his left arm under UKE's right arm and applies to UKE the UKI-GOSHI (Floating Loin) to the left (9 and 10).

UKE is extended, feet joined, on TORI's left hip and supports himself with his right hand on TORI's right hip or on his shoulder (11); then after having remained motionless for two or three seconds TORI lets UKE fall gently to the ground.

6th KATA—3rd Series

2.—MUNE-OSHI (To push back the chest)
Figs. 87 *and* 88

TORI and UKE at the end of the preceding movement are again on the axis of the Kata, TORI to the right and UKE to the left of the "Joseki", midway.

UKE bends his right arm, palm directed forward towards TORI whom he tries to push back on the left side of his chest with a gesture similar to the first movement of the 5th Kata (Itsutsu-no-Kata) (1 and 2).

TORI then seizes UKE's right wrist with his left hand "fork-wise" and pivots very slightly towards his left with his knees flexed (3).

Then in his turn he pushes UKE back with his right hand against the left part of the chest and UKE seizes TORI's right wrist with his left hand "fork-wise" (4).

UKE then lifts TORI's right wrist and lowers TORI's left wrist so as to grasp it over the top with his right hand (5).

TORI escapes this double hold of the wrists by pivoting a half turn to the right (6) which brings him back to back with UKE and enables him again to take hold of UKE's left wrist with his right hand; but UKE retains the hold with his right hand on TORI's left wrist (7).

At the moment when TORI and UKE are back to back TORI's right arm and UKE's left arm are raised diagonally and TORI's left arm and UKE's right arm are lowered as shown in Fig. 7.

But the movement of rotation is continued: TORI raises his left arm which always holds UKE's right hand at the wrist, and lowers his right arm the hand of which always holds UKE's left wrist (8).

Fig. 87

TORI and UKE are therefore again face to face after an entire rotation, to the right for TORI and to the left for UKE (9 and 12). TORI's hands have returned to grasp UKE's wrists from either side, the left hand operating as shown in the three diagrams underneath 10 and the right hand as shown in the three diagrams adjoining 11.

When TORI and UKE are in position 12, TORI encircles UKE's right leg with his right leg and places his right foot behind UKE's feet while his right hand descends as far as UKE's left elbow; then TORI breaks UKE's balance backwards (13).

At the end of a pause of two or three seconds TORI brings UKE back to the right natural posture.

Fig. 88

6th KATA—3rd Series

3.—TSUKI-AGE (Blow with fist from down upwards)
Figs 89 and 90

TORI and UKE are face to face on the axis of the Kata, midway, TORI to the right and UKE to the left of the "Joseki".

UKE recedes a step with his right foot and pivots a quarter turn to the right. At the same time he stretches out his right arm in the line of his shoulders, the palm in front and towards the ground, the fingers opened and stretched (1).

Fig. 89

Then UKE clenches his right fist progressively and advances a big step with his right foot which brings him close to TORI whom he tries to strike on the chin (2) with the approved upper-cut.

TORI dodges by receding a step with his left foot or only by bending backwards and flexing his knees a little. When UKE's right fist has passed his face and is approximately at the level of his forehead he covers it with the palm of his right hand (3).

TORI then pushes back UKE's fist towards his shoulder and TORI's left hand placed on UKE's right elbow completes this movement which tends to unbalance UKE backwards (4), and then to make him pivot to the left.

Fig. 90

UKE follows the movement; he pivots with a complete turn to the left and flexes his knees, his right arm in a large arc above his head (5).

TORI "maintains" UKE's rotation with his left hand which accompanies UKE's right elbow in its circular displacement. At the moment when UKE returns in front of TORI, TORI pushes UKE's right elbow with his left hand towards his right front (6).

UKE's right arm passes transversally in front of TORI's chest from left to right (7).

TORI advances his right arm which he places under UKE's forearm cross-wise (8).

He advances with a big step of his right foot which he brings behind UKE's feet and envelops his right leg. At the same time TORI blocks UKE's right deltoid in the hollow of his right elbow and presses his left palm against the upper part of UKE's right arm (9).

Lastly, TORI completes the hold and UKE's rear disequilibrium with the locking of his crossed forearms and his wrists (10) on the lines of the HADAKA-JIME (Naked Necklock) described on page 140 of the same author's *Judo*.

UKE signals his surrender after a few seconds by striking his thigh with his left hand and TORI brings him back to the normal posture.

Remark: It is not necessary to have an armlock; simply close contact suffices to control UKE's rear disequilibrium. Also TORI's left hand is simply placed above UKE's right elbow (10).

6th KATA—3rd Series

4.—UCHI-OROSHI (Blow with fist from above downwards) *Fig.* 91

UKE with his right forearm describes a circular movement: his open hand passes in front of his left shoulder and forehead, then descends again diagonally to the right. UKE then clenches his fist which he brings back before his right shoulder with his elbow completely bent. Lastly he raises his stretched arm above his shoulder (1).

TORI lowers his fist, the little-finger edge in front, towards the crown of TORI's head as he advances his right foot. TORI dodges by bending backwards or, if he is too near UKE, by retreating two short paces, first on the left, then on the right foot (2).

UKE's fist therefore passes in front of TORI's chest. When it reaches below the level of (TORI's) belt, TORI blocks UKE's wrist with his right hand "fork-wise" (3) and pushes it downwards as he advances with the tsugiashi, right foot first.

UKE pivots a quarter turn to the right and pushes back TORI's right elbow with his left hand, thumb on top (4).

TORI then describes a big circular movement with his right arm spirally forward towards the left (5). He thus executes a

Fig. 91

complete turn, seizes on the way with his left hand, thumb on the thumb edge, the left wrist of UKE who has followed his right elbow (6) and passes under UKE's left arm and armpit.

TORI is again behind UKE. He always keeps his left arm "T-shaped" with his left hand; passes his right forearm in front of UKE's neck as if to begin a rear strangulation, then recedes a step on his left foot in order to unbalance UKE clearly backwards (7).

UKE surrenders at the end of several seconds by striking his thigh with his right hand and TORI restores him to the natural posture.

Fig. 92

6th KATA—3rd Series

5.—RYOGAN-TSUKI (To stab the eyes) *Figs.* 92 *and* 93

The most usual initial position, TORI to the right facing UKE at a distance of about three steps.

UKE advances his right foot with his right arm stretched forward "T-shaped" at the level of the shoulder, the palm of the hand turned downwards (1). UKE's fingers should be arranged as far as possible like the diagram, which necessitates some training.

Fig. 93

UKE then aims at TORI's eyes. TORI pivots to the left and withdraws his left foot to elude the attack and seizes UKE's right wrist with his left hand, fingers on top (2).

TORI pushes forward UKE's left elbow with his right hand, fingers on top and stretched towards the left (4).

UKE pivots towards the left and TORI accompanies this gyration with his right hand (5 and 6).

UKE has returned in front of TORI who seizes his left sleeve
with his right hand and with his left hand now attacks him
also with a thrust to the eyes (7).

It is UKE's turn to dodge by pivoting a quarter turn to the
right and withdrawing his right foot, and to grasp TORI's
left wrist with his right hand, fingers on top (8).

This is a repetition of what has just been described: TORI
seizes UKE's right wrist with his right hand, fingers on top, to
extricate himself (9) and UKE in his turn pushes forward
TORI's right elbow with his left hand so as to make him pivot
to the left (10).

TORI pivots, as a matter of fact, but withdraws so as to
slide his left arm under the right armpit of UKE to whom he
applies the UKI-GOSHI (Floating Loin) to the left (11 and 12).

TORI at the end of several seconds gently replaces UKE on
the ground.

This movement terminates the 6th KATA. TORI and UKE
return to their respective initial positions, salute each other
standing, then salute standing the "Joseki".

It is advisable again to insist upon the necessity in the
execution of this Kata of adopting a slow, continuous, uniform,
follow-through rhythm which clearly demonstrates the circular
fluidity of the displacements and the systematic non-resistance
of the gestures, which will be better understood now that the
15 Movements comprising the JU-NO-KATA have been studied
a little.

VII

THE SEVENTH KATA
OR
KOSHIKI-NO-KATA
(Antique Kata)

The KOSHIKI-NO-KATA, or Antique Kata, originated from the KITO School, one of the most celebrated and most ancient Schools of old Jujutsu of Japan.

Professor KANO had studied Jujutsu in this School and later wished to preserve this Kata as the most representative of the distant origins of Judo, of the century-old techniques of the "Kumiuchi", the in-fighting of the samurai clad in feudal armour (yoroi), as the most characteristic of the tradition of the martial spirit of Japan.

For Jigoro KANO, if the KIME-NO-KATA constituted the preparatory training for combat, if the ITSUTSU-NO-KATA represented the supreme synthesis of the great principles of Judo, then the KOSHIKI-NO-KATA was the sum of these principles defined by tradition and experience during the centuries and expressed by the image of combat itself.

The KOSHIKI-NO-KATA is therefore the most vital, the truest, the closest approach to real combat, and that is undoubtedly the reason, at least as emotional as logical, why Professor KANO preferred this Kata.

While he was alive he always liked to be the only one to demonstrate it as TORI, wearing the black ceremonial "hakama" (loose trousers with many folds in front) *de rigueur* on such occasions, with either Yoshiaki YAMASHITA or Hajime ISOGAI, both 10th Dan and now deceased, in the role of UKE.

The 7th Kata is therefore the superior Kata *par excellence* which only great experts are properly qualified to execute.

It comprises numerous forms of throws many of which are sutemis, because the demonstrators are supposed to be clad in feudal armour, or Yoroi which renders their tai-sabaki rigid and artificial like the displacement of an automaton.

The performers should evoke also the atmosphere of true combat which they are supposed to deliver, at one and the same time noble and implacable.

The KOSHIKI-NO-KATA is composed of two Series and includes 21 throws in all.

The 1st Series OMOTE (from the front and fundamental in its figurative sense) comprises 14 movements. It should be executed at a rather slow and staccato pace, with the pauses between each throw well marked.

The 2nd Series URA (from behind, application in a figurative sense) includes 7 movements. It should be executed more rapidly and without wasted time.

It should be noted that the 14 movements of the 1st Series are grouped two by two, each technical pair being the complement of the uneven number which precedes it.

SEVENTH KATA
(21 *Movements*)

1st Series—*OMOTE* (14 *movements*) (*from the front or fundamental form*)

1. TAI: Starting posture
2. YUME-NO-UCHI: The dream
3. RYOKUHI: To master his strength
4. MIZU-GURUMA: The water-wheel
5. MIZU-NAGARE: The stream
6. HIKI-OTOSHI: To pull and make fall
7. KODAORE: The tree-trunk
8. UCHI-KUDAKI: To pulverize
9. TANI-OTOSHI: The fall in the valley
10. KURUMA-DAOSHI: The thrown-down wheel
11. SHIKORO-DORI: Hold on shoulder-piece (of armour)
12. SHIKORO-GAESHI: Overturning by shoulder-piece
13. YUDACHI: Evening rain
14. TAKI-OTOSHI: The cascade

2nd Series—*URA* (7 *movements*) (*the reverse or derived from*)

1. MI-KUDAKI: To reduce the body to powder
2. KURUMA-GAESHI: To revolve like a wheel
3. MIZU-IRI: To follow the current
4. RYU-SETSU: The snow on the willow
5. SAKA-OTOSHI: To throw down on the slope
6. YUKI-ORE: The branch broken under the weight of the snow
7. IWA-NAMI: The wave against the rock

1.—TAI (Starting Position) *Fig.* 94

Fig. 94

In the traditional demonstration of the 7th KATA, TORI is to the left and UKE to the right of the "Joseki".

Unlike the ITSUTSU-NO-KATA, which is more spectacular in the non-traditional arrangement of TORI to the right and UKE to the left on the axis of the Kata, in relation to the "Joseki", the KOSHIKI-NO-KATA must be demonstrated in the ritual form which distinguishes it from the six other Katas, TORI being to the left and UKE to the right in the initial posture.

The Salutation is made ritually by descending on the heels, then placing both knees together on the ground and afterwards rising to one's feet. Actually the standing salutation is allowed in the ordinary demonstration. The reason for the ceremonial salutation executed in the particular manner above described is that the demonstrators are supposed to be clad in the rigid feudal armour known as "Yoroi".

Consequently, TORI to the left and UKE to the right salute the "Joseki" standing; then they salute each other either standing or in ceremonial fashion.

TORI pivots a quarter turn to the right and takes a step forward with his left foot, then his right, to place himself in the starting posture (1).

UKE starts with the left foot and advances diagonally towards TORI, a little in front of him. When UKE's right foot reaches just in front of TORI's left foot, UKE seizes TORI's belt in front with his left hand and from behind with his right hand in the normal hold, his thumbs on top, then raises his left leg at a right-angle (2 seen in front and 2A seen from behind the back of TORI) and raises himself a little on the tips of his right foot.

UKE brings back his left leg towards the ground and takes advantage of this impetus to try to throw TORI with a hip movement. TORI blocks UKE's left hip with his left hand and pushes UKE backwards at the level of his left collar-bone with the palm of his right hand (3).

TORI then falls back with short staccato steps towards his left back in the direction of UKE's disequilibrium which is also the axis of his approach to TORI (sometimes TORI unbalances UKE direct lateral left).

Suddenly TORI lets himself drop on to his right knee and throws UKE who falls on his back at TORI's left back (4).

TORI then assumes the high kneeling posture of the Kata, and for this purpose brings his left foot flush with the mat towards the outside of an angle of about 30 degrees so that the planes of his legs are at a right-angle. UKE, however, sits down again slowly, his legs separated almost at a right-angle and with his hands on his knees, thumbs and fingers joined inwards (5).

Lastly, TORI and UKE slowly rise to their feet together without placing their hands on the ground but pressing them on their knees, and resume the initial position (1). Do not forget that the movement which follows is the complement of that which has just been described.

Remark: In theory the guiding idea of this throw is that TORI places his knee so that UKE's fall is made transversally on his head, thus causing a fracture of the spine.

2.—YUME-NO-UCHI (The Dream) *Fig.* 95

Fig. 95

Exactly the same beginning of the movement (1 and 2) as for the preceding one.

But this time UKE resists with his "hara" (abdomen) by blocking his abdominals. TORI immediately takes advantage of this to pass round his right hip and recede always with short staccato steps in order to unbalance him forward (3) and finally throw him (4) with the sutemi YOKO-GURUMA (Lateral Wheel) but TORI's legs should remain in front of UKE's right leg. (*Translator's Note:* In the illustration only TORI's right leg is shown in front of UKE's right leg.)

UKE executes a frontal rolling fall which brings him to his feet, the feet side by side, but TORI remains two or three seconds on his back, arms crossed and legs separated at about 60 degrees (5), then slowly regains his feet.

Remark: There exists between the 1st and 2nd movements of the 7th Kata the same concatenation as between the 2nd movement of the 4th Series and the 2nd movement of the 5th Series of the 1st Kata, respectively URA-NAGE (Rear Throw) and YOKO-GURUMA (Lateral Wheel), according to whether UKE's resistance is frontal or backward. In this movement the general direction of TORI's body should indicate the axis of UKE's fall. In order to regain his feet TORI should first squat on his heels, then draw himself up by stretching both legs at the same time and not one after the other. This observation holds good every time TORI and UKE are on the ground, whatever their positions may be, and they must resume standing.

7th KATA—1st Series

3.—RYOKUHI (To master his strength)
Fig. 96

TORI places himself on the axis of the Kata and in right profile to the "Joseki". UKE passes round him on his left flank and therefore without coming between the "Joseki" and him, and takes his position facing TORI in left profile (1) at a distance of a little more than a yard.

UKE takes a step with his left foot, then advances his right foot and seizes TORI's belt with extended arms and crossed wrists, the right above the left (2).

TORI dodges by withdrawing a step with his right foot and pivoting a little towards his right. He seizes UKE's right wrist with his left hand, his thumb at the side of UKE's thumb and places his right hand on the outer surface of UKE's right elbow (3).

TORI then with a combined movement of both his hands and crossed forearms, the right above the left, amplifies UKE's frontal disequilibrium. He takes advantage of this to place himself behind UKE and up against him. TORI's right hand ascends along UKE's right arm as far as his shoulder. The palm of TORI's left hand presses on UKE's left arm and pectorals (4).

UKE re-establishes his equilibrium with a tendency through reaction to slight backward disequilibrium. TORI then brings

Fig. 96

him forward from his right flank, then unbalances him clearly and violently towards his right back where he throws him outright by letting himself fall on his left knee (5).

TORI brings his right foot outwards. UKE seats himself. Then both slowly rise to their feet according to the customary procedure, characteristic of the 7th Kata.

7th KATA—1st Series

4.—MIZU-GURUMA (The Water Wheel) *Fig.* 97

Fig. 97

Exactly the same starting movement as for the preceding one, since we are here concerned, as already said, with the complementary movement and disequilibrium (1 and 2).

TORI has amplified UKE's frontal disequilibrium as previously. UKE reacts and stands erect again behind, but TORI has let his right hand descend to UKE's right wrist which he pushes back upwards before his face. UKE's right forearm is therefore pressing transversely against his forehead (3).

TORI then places the palm of his left hand against the left hip of UKE whom he draws towards himself by continuing to push UKE's right forearm backwards (4). TORI has therefore advanced his left foot behind UKE's feet and tries to break UKE's balance backwards.

But UKE resists from his abdomen. TORI immediately takes advantage of UKE's frontal reaction and throws him forward with a turning movement similar to the YOKO-GURUMA (Lateral Wheel) or YOKO-WAKARE (Lateral Separation) already applied for the 2nd movement of this Series. Here also, as in all the throws of this kind executed in the 7th KATA, TORI's legs must remain side by side and on the same outward side of UKE's right leg (5 and 6).

UKE makes a very long rolling forward fall and comes to his feet, both feet on the same plane. TORI remains stretched on his back two or three seconds and then slowly rises to his feet.

7th KATA—1st Series

5.—MIZU-NAGARE (The Brook) *Fig.* 98

TORI and UKE are on the axis of the Kata at a distance of about ten feet from each other, TORI to the right and UKE to the left of the "Joseki". Sometimes for the execution of this movement TORI and UKE place themselves diagonally.

TORI and UKE walk towards each other with slow and majestic steps. TORI stops at the moment when UKE is two paces away from him. UKE, however, makes a gesture as if to take a dagger from his belt against his right hip with his right hand and stretches out his left arm towards the lapels of TORI's collar in order to grip them and thus better ensure his thrust (1).

TORI slightly bends the upper part of his body backwards in order to dodge the attack which compels UKE to lean forward since his object is to take support on TORI's collar. TORI then seizes UKE's left wrist with his right hand in the normal hold and pulls it forward and downwards; the palm of TORI's left hand presses on the hollow of UKE's elbow, the thumb and fingers directed rather upwards (2).

TORI recedes with a big step on his right foot, lets himself suddenly fall on his right knee and throws UKE before him to his right (3).

UKE falls on his back and pivots towards his right. He seats himself and turns his back on TORI since his fall has led him to make a half turn. TORI has not this time brought his left foot towards the outside (4) because he has at once taken the high kneeling posture in equilibrium; then Tori and Uke slowly rise to their feet without making a pause.

Remark: Uke must on no account make a Kata fall but simply let himself go in the direction of his disequilibrium.

Fig. 98

7th KATA—1st Series

6.—HIKI-OTOSHI (To pull and make fall) *Fig.* 99

Tori and Uke are in their respective positions, the opposite to those of the preceding movement, Tori to the left and Uke to the right of the "Joseki", at three paces from each other on the axis of the Kata (or if really necessary diagonally).

UKE walks towards TORI, his right hand in front directed towards TORI's left shoulder and his left hand a little behind

Fig. 99

directed towards TORI's right armpit with the intention of unbalancing him and making him pivot and swing towards his right back (1).

TORI pivots a quarter turn to the left, seizes UKE's right wrist with his left hand in the normal hold, presses the palm of his right hand in the hollow of UKE's right elbow (2), recedes with a big step of his left foot (3), lets himself drop on his left knee and suddenly throws UKE in the direction of his frontal disequilibrium (4).

This is therefore the symmetrical movement of the preceding one. TORI, as previously, at once places himself in the
high balanced kneeling posture, i.e. the planes of both his
legs at a right-angle. He has not therefore to separate his right
knee; he does not mark the pause. UKE sits down again also
without marking the characteristic pause (5); then TORI and
UKE slowly rise to their feet.

Fig. 100

7th KATA—1st Series

7.—KODAORE (The tree-trunk) *Fig.* 100

TORI to the right, UKE to the left, at a distance of about
12 feet on the axis of the Kata.

They walk towards each other, then having arrived at three paces UKE waits for TORI who lifts his extended right arm with the hand held "blade-wise", as if to strike UKE on the forehead (1).

UKE dodges by withdrawing his right foot and pivoting a quarter turn to the right. At the same time he grasps TORI's right wrist with his right hand in the normal hold, fingers on top (2).

TORI has his right foot advanced behind UKE's left heel. UKE tries to take advantage of TORI's advance to apply a hip movement to him, but TORI pushes his right arm in front of UKE's face and resists with his abdominals, and with his left hand, thumb on top, grasps UKE's belt against his left hip (3).

UKE marks his rear disequilibrium by receding a small step and bends backwards supported on TORI's right hip. TORI then lets himself suddenly drop on his left knee thus throwing UKE on to his back towards his right back (4). In this movement TORI's right palm is turned towards the ground because the hands must always accompany and express with their gestures the movements of the body and reflect the harmony of the whole.

UKE seats himself again and TORI separates his right knee after having marked a slight pause before letting his right arm fall back and placing his hand on his knee.

TORI and UKE preserve their attitude two or three seconds and then slowly rise to their feet.

Remark: Here as each time that TORI is supposed to throw UKE on the tip of his knee UKE's fall is longer and is made after a retreat of several staccato steps on his heels to avoid and get round TORI's knee.

7th KATA—1st Series

8.—UCHI-KUDAKI (To pulverize) *Fig.* 101

Initial position the reverse of that of the preceding movement, TORI to the left and UKE to the right, at a distance of about 12 feet on the axis of the Kata.

TORI and UKE advance towards each other, always with slow steps; then at a distance of six feet UKE stops and awaits TORI who walks towards him progressively raising his extended left arm and the hand held "blade-wise" and fingers joined to give UKE a thrust (tegatana) to the solar-plexus (1).

UKE dodges as previously but symmetrically, i.e. by pivoting a quarter turn to the left this time and withdrawing his left foot. At the same time UKE seizes TORI's left wrist with his left hand in the normal hold, fingers on top (2).

Fig. 101

UKE then advances his right foot in front of TORI to apply a hip throw to him. Immediately TORI passes his left arm transversally in front of UKE's chest and takes hold of UKE's belt against his right hip with his right hand, fingers underneath (3).

UKE is unbalanced towards his left back. He bends backwards and takes support on TORI's left hip and recedes a small step on his left foot. TORI further emphasizes the contact of his hip, then suddenly lets himself drop on his right knee after several short trailing steps. UKE falls to the left behind TORI (4).

UKE seats himself again. TORI separates his left knee (5). Both mark a pause of two or three seconds and then rise to their feet.

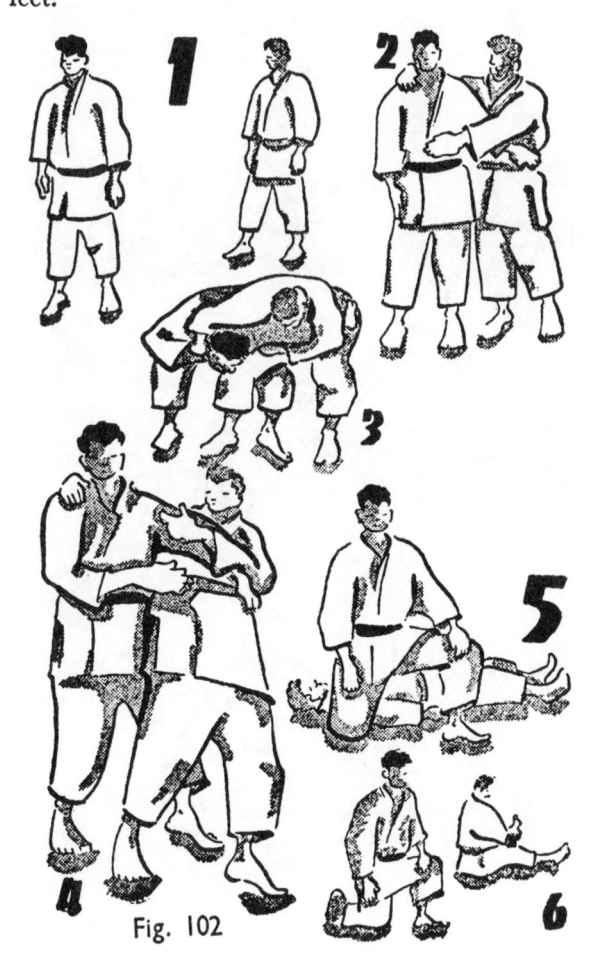

Fig. 102

7th KATA—1st Series

9.—TANI-OTOSHI (The fall in the valley) *Fig.* 102

TORI is facing the "Joseki" and UKE is standing about six feet behind him diagonally to his left (1). Their respective positions are therefore somewhat similar to those of the start of the first movement.

UKE bends his steps towards TORI and places himself against his left flank rather behind. He then pushes TORI to compel him to bend forward, and presses the palm of his right hand on TORI's right shoulder and his left hand in front at the level of TORI's belt (2). TORI's left hand "in reverse" rests on UKE's left hip in front.

TORI bends forward under this double pushing in a contrary direction, with the upper part of his body parallel to the ground. At this moment the action of UKE's right hand becomes inoperative. TORI seizes the fingers of this hand with his right hand, thumb underneath against the palm, as if to drag UKE forward and throw him over his shoulder. UKE resists by advancing his right foot in front of TORI's feet (3).

Then UKE stands erect again behind to return to the right natural posture, but TORI controls the movement and places his left foot behind UKE's left heel so that UKE is again bent backwards and supported on TORI's left hip with his bust held under TORI's armpit and left arm. TORI then places his right hand against the front of UKE's right hip (4) to complete the contact and disequilibrium. (Sometimes TORI with his right hand lifts UKE's right arm above his head).

TORI makes UKE retreat with several small, rapid and staccato steps; then lets himself drop on his right knee and throws UKE on to his back towards his left back (5).

TORI separates his left knee and UKE sits down again (6). Then both slowly rise again to their feet.

7th KATA—1st Series

10.—KURUMA-DAOSHI (The thrown down wheel)
Fig. 103

Almost the same start of movement as the preceding one, but UKE comes against TORI's left flank, tries to make him pivot and unbalance him towards his left back by pushing his right shoulder with his right hand and pulling him on the left pectoral with his left hand (1 and 2).

TORI follows the movement but remains upright and finds himself again after a half turn to the left facing UKE. He then slips his right hand under UKE's left armpit and makes him "float" unbalanced forward on his toes (3).

Then TORI retreats and with a circular movement (4 and 5)

throws UKE according to the technique already utilized in this Kata, viz., the sutemi YOKO-WAKARE.

UKE executes a rolling frontal fall over TORI in order to regain his feet in the natural posture (6). TORI remains two or three seconds on his back and then slowly stands up again.

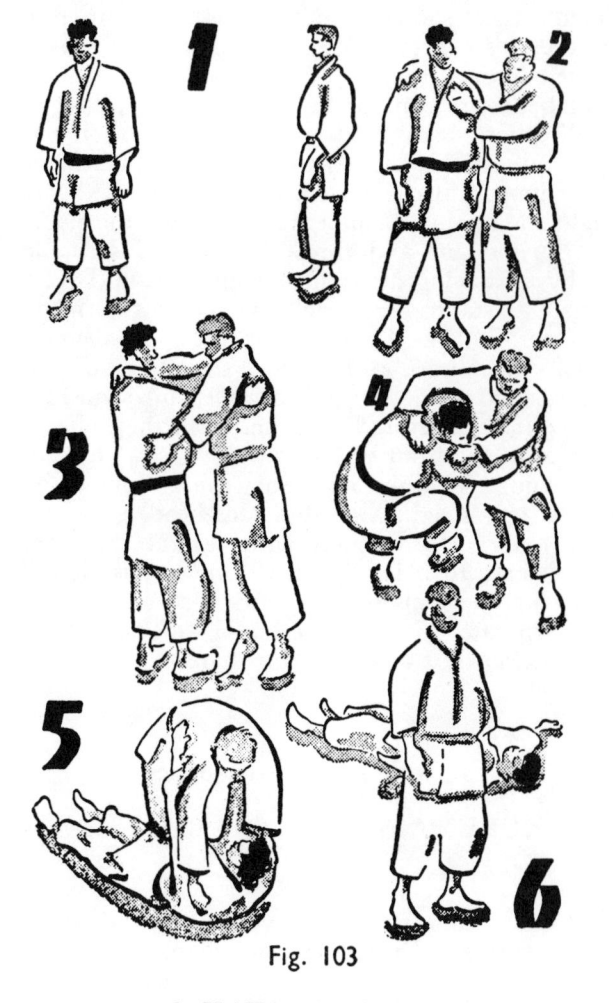

Fig. 103

7th KATA—1st Series

11.—SHIKORO-DORI (Hold on shoulder-piece)
Fig. 104

TORI to the right, UKE to the left on the axis of the Kata at two paces from each other.

UKE advances his left foot and stretches his left arm to take hold of the front of TORI's belt (1).

TORI dodges by pivoting a quarter turn to the left and withdrawing his left foot. At the same time he seizes with his

Fig. 104

right hand, thumb on top, UKE's wrist which he pulls in the direction of his (UKE's) advance and the palm of his left hand covers UKE's chin (2).

TORI makes UKE's head turn towards his right back which contributes to UKE's loss of equilibrium. When UKE's right foot "floats", his back is turned to TORI who places his right hand on UKE's right shoulder (3 and 4).

TORI lets himself suddenly drop on his left knee and throws UKE towards his right back on to his back (5).

TORI separates his right knee. UKE sits up again (6). There is a pause of two or three seconds and they both rise slowly to their feet.

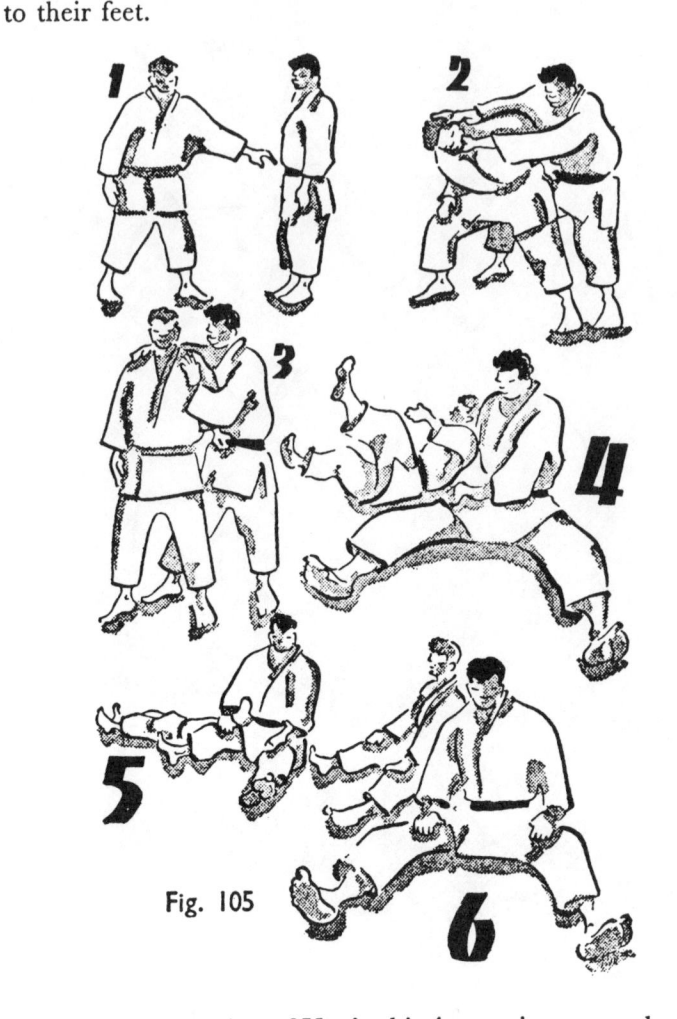

Fig. 105

Remark: The torsion of UKE's chin is very important because it recalls the ancient methods of combat in feudal armour, viz., the torsion of the chin-piece of the helmet, shoulder-piece, &c. and because it emphasizes the incapacity which one experiences to retain one's sense of balance when one's head is suddenly displaced and one's gaze has no longer a guide-mark.

7th KATA—1st Series

12.—SHIKORO-GAESHI (Overturning by shoulder-piece)
Fig. 105

The same start as for the preceding movement. This time UKE actually seizes the front of TORI's belt (1) with his left hand, thumb underneath.

Then UKE tries to apply to TORI a hip throw to the left but TORI blocks with his abdomen, advances his right leg and with both hands seizes UKE's head on which he inflicts a torsion from right to left (2).

UKE, then unbalanced towards his right, resists and stands erect again. But TORI's left hand quits UKE's chin to press against his left pectoral, and TORI's right hand quits the crown of UKE's head to place itself on UKE's right shoulder (3).

TORI lets himself suddenly with a single movement drop directly seated on the spot, without stepping back, and forcibly throws UKE towards his right back (4 and 5).

TORI and UKE remain two or three seconds in the usual seated posture, legs separated, hands on knees (6) and then rise slowly together to their feet.

7th KATA—1st Series

13.—YUDACHI (Evening Rain) *Fig.* 106

TORI to the right, UKE to the left, midway.

TORI with both hands takes hold of both UKE's lapels, right hand on the left lapel and left hand on the right lapel (1).

Then TORI with the help of his left hand takes hold of both of UKE's lapels with his right hand alone, but places his index finger between the lapels to strengthen his hold (2).

UKE advances his left foot and with his left hand seizes TORI's right sleeve (3).

TORI then withdraws his left foot when UKE advances his right foot and stretches his right arm to encircle TORI's waist with a view to applying to him a hip throw (4) but without succeeding.

TORI with his left hand has taken hold of UKE's right sleeve; he pivots a quarter turn to the left, lets himself drop on his left knee and throws UKE with the UKI-OTOSHI (Floating Drop) (5), but UKE should make a lateral fall, pivoted on his right heel, and not a forward Kata fall as in the 1st KATA.

TORI should have instantly taken the high kneeling posture (6) when he threw UKE. He makes a beat with his right hand on his knee as UKE sits up again (7); then both rise to their feet.

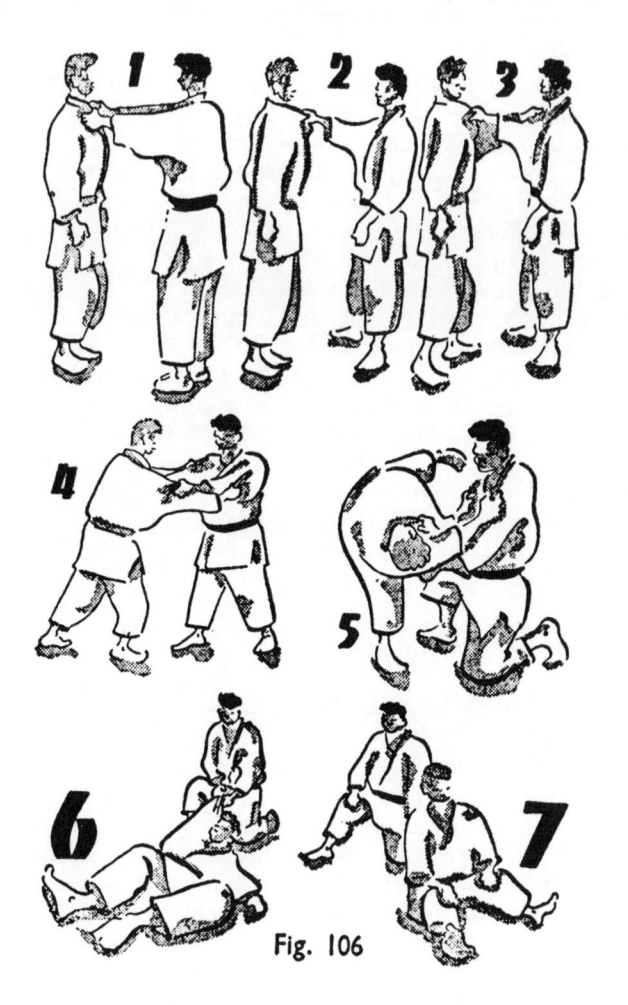

Fig. 106

7th KATA—1st Series

14.—TAKI-OTOSHI (The Cascade) *Fig.* 107

Exactly the same starting movement as the preceding one to arrive at 1.

UKE with his left hand seizes (TORI's) right sleeve and advances his left foot. TORI withdraws his right foot.

UKE then advances his right foot and passing his right arm over TORI's left arm presses his right hand against TORI's back in contemplation of throwing TORI with a hip throw (2). TORI with his left hand takes hold of the middle of UKE's belt behind his waist (or simply presses it with the palm of his hand).

Fig. 107

TORI then places his feet behind those of UKE and thus breaks UKE's balance behind (3).

But UKE resists with his abdomen and bends forward. Immediately TORI swings towards his left back with a half turn and throws UKE with a variant of the YOKO-WAKARE (4 and 5).

Uke makes a rolling fall which brings him to his feet. Tori remains on his back a few moments in the customary posture, arms crossed and feet separated, and then rises slowly to his feet.

This throw terminates the 1st Series "Omote" of the Koshiki-no-Kata.

Fig. 108

7th KATA—2nd Series

1.—MI-KUDAKI (To reduce the body to powder)
Fig. 108

In this Series the rhythm of the displacements and throws is much more rapid, the pace more supple, less majestic and solemn, and above all there is absolutely no pause between the seven movements which follow; they must succeed one another like the model demonstration of Randori.

The same starting posture as for the 1st Movement of the

Fig. 109

1st Series: TORI to the left facing the "Joseki", UKE to the right, diagonally back (1).

UKE with both hands takes hold of TORI's belt in front and behind as in the 1st Movement of the 1st Series and lifts his left leg at a right angle. But at the moment when he brings back his leg to the ground with impetus in order to attempt to throw TORI with a hip throw, TORI with his right hand in the normal hold, fingers on top, seizes the left wrist of UKE whom he thus compels to relinquish the hold on his (TORI's) belt. TORI then lifts UKE's left arm transversally in front of his chest and slips his left forearm under UKE's left armpit (2).

TORI then begins to unbalance UKE backwards towards his left (3).

But UKE resists with his abdomen and bends forward. TORI immediately takes advantage of this to transform UKE's back disequilibrium into a frontal one and throws UKE as he swings with a half turn to the left on his back according to the YOKO-WAKARE technique already employed (4 and 5).

UKE executes a rolling forward fall and TORI immediately gets up so that they are again face to face, UKE to the left, TORI to the right for the execution of the following movement.

7th KATA—2nd Series

2.—KURUMA-GAESHI (To pivot like a wheel)
Fig. 109

UKE to the left of the axis of the Kata at the close of the preceding movement rushes headlong on TORI, his arms extended and his hands in front, to push against his shoulders, rather like the 1st Movement of the 4th Series of the 1st KATA (NAGE-NO-KATA) i.e. the TOMOE-NAGE, or Stomach Throw (1).

TORI immediately yields to the push; he lets himself go on to his back and passes his legs side by side to the outside of UKE's right foot and placing his hands on both sides under UKE's armpits (2), with a combined movement of the wrists, throws him over and behind him (3).

UKE makes a forward fall towards the right end of the axis of the Kata and again rises to his feet at the same time as TORI.

7th KATA—2nd Series

3.—MIZU-IRI (To follow the current) *Fig.* 110

UKE runs towards TORI with his right arm extended with the object of violently pushing his left shoulder (1).

TORI seizes UKE's wrist or forearm with his left hand and the inner part of the arm with his right hand (2).

Then he lets himself go on to his back and thus throws UKE diagonally over him (3).

UKE executes a forward fall towards the left of the axis of the Kata. TORI and UKE again regain their feet at the same time.

Fig. 110

7th KATA—2nd Series

4.—RYU-SETSU (The Snow on the Willow) *Fig.* 111

TORI runs towards UKE who has finished his preceding forward fall, and with his right hand makes a feint ("kasumi") to the face. Arrived quite close to UKE he thrusts his fingers pointed forward and upwards in the direction of UKE's eyes and forehead (with the gesture as of throwing, for example, a handful of sand). UKE instinctively withdraws his head backwards and upwards (1).

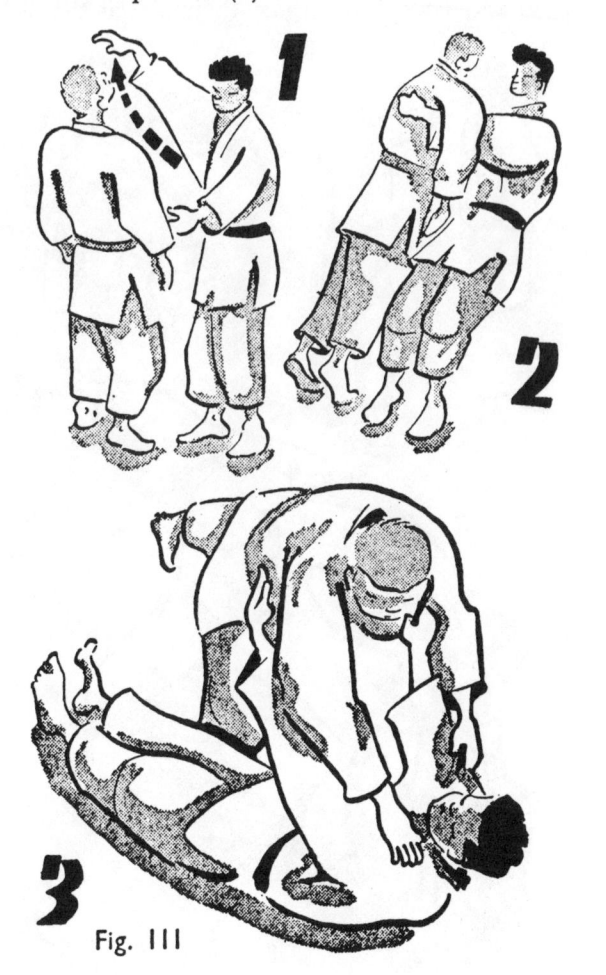

Fig. 111

When UKE brings his head back to the front TORI takes hold of his left lapel with his right hand and places his left hand under UKE's right armpit (2).

Then TORI lets himself go backwards on to his back, slides his feet to the outside of Uke's right foot and throws him over and behind himself diagonally (3).

Remark: "Kasumi" means in Japanese fog, mist or haze. In this context it means a feint. When made with one hand it is called "katate-kasumi", or with both hands "ryote-kasumi". It is designed to disturb and frighten the adversary so as to distract his attention in order to attack him with greater efficacy.

Fig. 112

7th KATA—2nd Series

5.—SAKA-OTOSHI (To throw down on the slope)
Fig. 112

UKE advances his left foot and attacks TORI, his left hand pointed in front as though to stab him with a dagger (1).

TORI withdraws his right foot, pivots towards his right and with his right hand seizes either the left wrist or the sleeve of UKE on the forearm, and with his right (? left) hand the top of the arm or the inner part of the sleeve (2).

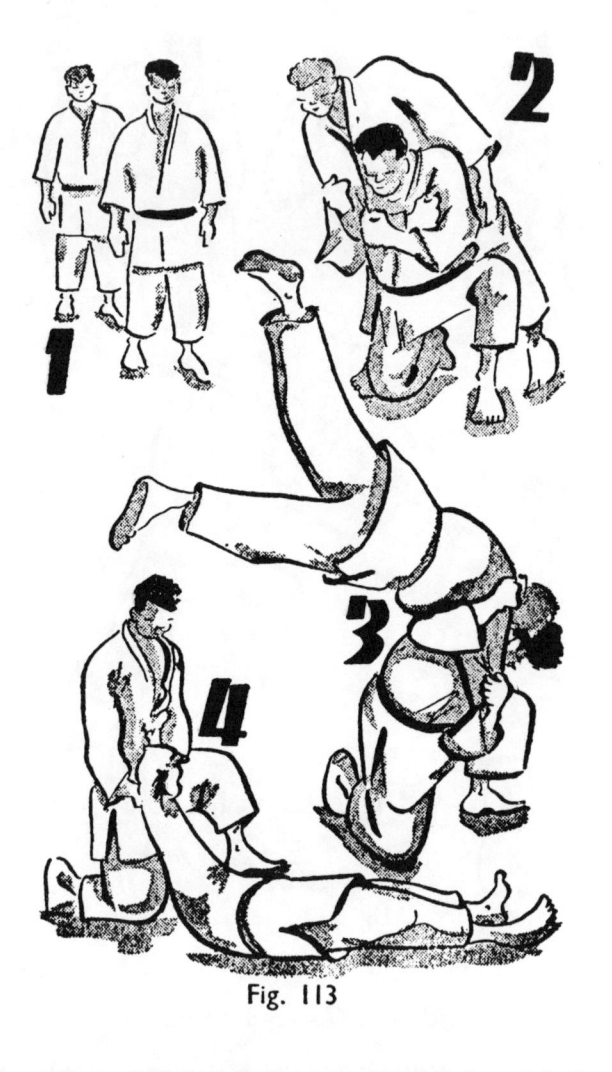

Fig. 113

TORI pulls and "winds" downwards and forward the (left) arm of UKE who falls as he pivots on his left heel (3 and 4).

TORI begins to walk slowly towards one of the ends of the (axis) of the Kata, in principle the right, and turns his back on UKE who rapidly rises to his feet (5).

7th KATA—2nd Series

6.—YUKI-ORE (The branch breaks under the weight of the snow) *Fig.* 113

UKE rushes at TORI who walks in front of him (1) and begins to encircle his shoulders with his arms as in the 8th Movement of the 2nd Series of the 4th KATA (KIME-NO-KATA).

TORI then executes the same counter: he lets himself drop on his right knee, the foot between those of UKE, and throws UKE with a shoulder movement, a variant of the SEOI-OTOSHI (Shoulder Drop) (2 and 3).

UKE does a Kata fall to the right end of the axis of the Kata (4).

Remark: UKE may also do a fall pivoted around TORI's right shoulder and not over it.

7th KATA—2nd Series

7.—IWA-NAMI (The Wave against the Rocks) *Fig.* 114

At the moment when UKE gets up and turns towards TORI, the latter makes a feint with both hands, "ryote-kasumi", at his face (1).

Immediately TORI seizes both UKE's lapels on both sides of his neck (2) and when UKE brings his head forward TORI throws him with the classic or standard Sutemi of the 7th KATA, both his legs sliding to the outside of UKE's right foot (3).

This throw terminates the execution of the KOSHIKI-NO-KATA. TORI and UKE rise to their feet again, repair to their initial places, face each other, readjust their judogi, salute each other as at the beginning, then turn towards the "Joseki" which they also salute standing.

———

After a preliminary study of the KOSHIKI-NO-KATA we can better understand the reasons for the names of the two Series of which it is composed.

OMOTE, as we know, signifies "from the front, direct", and

in a figurative sense "fundamental". The 14 movements of this Series begin in fact with direct attacks, even when they are preceded by lateral approaches, and are grouped two by two symmetrically in fundamental techniques.

Fig. 114

URA means "reverse, in a contrary direction, overturning, from behind, or behind", and in a figurative sense "variant, application, derived".

The seven movements of this Series constitute a randori of rapid application of the basic techniques of the 1st Series and almost all the throws are made in sutemi, TORI falling down backwards.

CONCLUSION

We have now reached the end of this study of the seven fundamental Katas of Judo. It is worth while, by way of conclusion, to give a few words of advice even at the risk of repeating what has already been said.

All the Kata movements are at first simple, natural and logical. Shun the artificial and discover the reasons for all the gestures which you execute in the course of the demonstration of a Kata. It is not sufficient that these reasons are explained to you by your instructor; you must find them again yourself.

At the start of the study of a Kata analyse well the movements in slow motion down to the smallest details; then go progressively more swiftly until the normal speed of execution is reached.

Train often all alone "with your shadow" to repeat all the movements of all the Katas.

Always preserve a good balance, a good attitude, a fundamental displacement.

Make your entire body participate in the movement.

Accustom yourself to breathe very deeply before beginning each Series of a Kata, or even each movement.

Don't run about uselessly under the pretext of "not turning your back on the Joseki". The truest road is the simplest, often the most direct. Remember only that it is more appropriate not to turn one's back on the "Joseki" before and during the action, i.e. during the preparation and at the beginning of the execution of the movement. But there is no absolute rule; it is a matter of spirit rather than of form which depends upon each specific case.

Lastly the detailed figures in successive phases require few indicatory arrows of the direction of the movements presumed to be already known, but the numbers will facilitate for you the reading and the grouping and will enable you rapidly to review the concatenation of the holds when you have attentively read the explanatory text.